TRY OUR APP

It's easy to keep up on every issue of BLOCK magazine. Access it from all your devices. And when you subscribe to BLOCK, it's free with your subscription! For the app search BLOCK magazine in the app store. Available for both Apple and Android.

EXECUTIVE EDITORS
Mike Mifsud, Alan Doan, Jenny Doan, Sarah Galbraith, David Mifsud

MANAGING EDITOR
Natalie Earnheart

CREATIVE DIRECTOR
Christine Ricks

PHOTOGRAPHY TEAM
Mike Brunner, Lauren Dorton, Jennifer Dowling, Dustin Weant

PATTERN TEAM
Tyler MacBeth, Jessica Toye, Denise Lane,

PROJECT DESIGN TEAM
Jenny Doan, Natalie Earnheart

EDITORS & COPYWRITERS
Camille Maddox, Nichole Spravzoff, David Litherland

SEWIST TEAM
Jenny Doan, Natalie Earnheart, Carol Henderson, Janice Richardson

QUILTING & BINDING DEPARTMENT
Becky Bowen, Glenda Rorabough, Nikki LaPiana, Amy Turpin, Debbie Elder, Holly Clevenger, Kristen Cash, Todd Harman, Jessica Paup, Jan Meek, Linda Frump, Franny Fleming, Rachael Joyce, Selena Smiley, Nora Clutter, Lyndia Lovell, Jackie Jones, Roxanna Hinkle, Deloris Burnett, Bernice Kelley, Darlene Smith, Janet Yamamoto

LOCATION CREDIT
Mari's House B&B Hamilton, MO
Fran Esry Home, Smithville, MO
Anne Crawford Home, Hamilton, MO
Kyle and Cheyanne Hefley Home, Lawson MO
The Hangout Eatery, Hamilton MO
The Tree Patch, Hamilton MO

PRINTING COORDINATORS
Rob Stoebener, Seann Dwyer

PRINTING SERVICES
Walsworth Print Group
803 South Missouri
Marceline, MO 64658

CONTACT US
Missouri Star Quilt Company
114 N Davis
Hamilton, MO 64644
888-571-1122
info@missouriquiltco.com

content

Oops! Sometimes we make mistakes.
To find corrections to every issue of Block
go to: **www.msqc.co/corrections**

hello

Preparation isn't about perfectionism. To me, it's more about allowing myself to enjoy important moments without the thought, *What if?* I recently heard a wonderful quote by Brené Brown that has stuck with me: "I don't have to chase extraordinary moments to find happiness—it's right in front of me if I'm paying attention and practicing gratitude." Every day of our lives can be extraordinary if we're noticing all the amazing things happening, even on the smallest scale. It's my goal to live my life with intent, recognizing all the good things around me and the kind things people do, while preparing for the future with purpose. Not all good things are serendipitous; sometimes we must cling to them with all our might for them to come into being, but I believe our intentions really do matter. If we believe in something, we can help bring it to pass in time through hard work and perseverance.

As the summer winds down, the faintest whisper of a cool breeze or one red leaf on a green tree reminds me of all the exciting celebrations to come toward the end of the year. Preparing for them now allows me to relax and be present later on, knowing I've done my best to make a plan (that will most likely change!). My hope is these holiday projects will inspire you and help you to celebrate all of the little, remarkable moments of life. Adding your own personal touch makes them even more memorable. And remember, as you create your own beautiful quilts and handmade projects, allow them to be human. Don't agonize about a stitch out of place. Allow it to remind you of its origin and embrace your humanity. It's what makes you and everything you make truly unique.

Jenny

JENNY DOAN
MISSOURI STAR QUILT CO.

For the tutorial and everything
you need to make this quilt visit:
www.msqc.co/holidayblock19

christmas tree pinwheel

Giving gifts is sometimes the hardest part of the Christmas season. You always want the gift to be thoughtful, and for it to be something the giftee will really enjoy, but sometimes you just get stumped! Other times, you'll see something in the store or online, and immediately know that it will make the perfect gift for that special someone. Of course, they always say that great minds think alike, and that can lead to some very funny Christmas mornings, as Dedra and her family learned firsthand.

One of Dedra's most treasured memories growing up was her mother, Donna, reading *Little House on the Prairie* by Laura Ingalls Wilder as a bedtime story for her and her sister. Laura's life on the American frontier had always sparked Dedra's imagination; while other girls her age played house, Dedra and her sister would pretend to be out on the Great Plains, living like Laura. When the television show was made, she devoured every episode.

This love for *Little House on the Prairie* spread out throughout the family, and Dedra passed this love on to her children, nieces, and nephews as well. So, it was no surprise when, while Christmas shopping a few years back, Dedra found the perfect gift for her mother. A big book chain had released leather bound editions of many famous books including, it turns out, a beautiful copy of Laura Ingalls Wilder's collected stories. The moment she saw it, Dedra quickly grabbed one and knew that she had Christmas in the bag! Dedra wrapped the book with care, labeled "For: Mom Love: Dedra," and placed it under the tree, excited to see her mother's face light up when she opened it Christmas morning.

In the early morning light on Christmas Day, while the kids all ate treats from their stockings and the grownups sipped their coffee while wrapped up in holiday quilts, they began distributing presents. Donna picked up a book-shaped package, and Dedra could barely contain her excitement. Just as she had expected, Donna was overjoyed by the present! But, instead of thanking Dedra, she leaned over and hugged her sister instead.

Dedra, confused, picked up the discarded paper and looked at the label. "To: Mom From: your daughter Deneé." Her sister had bought their mom a copy as well! Dedra laughed as she retrieved her copy from under the tree and handed it to her mom, letting her know what happened. They all laughed at the coincidence, but then Dedra's daughter dropped a suspiciously book-shaped present on her lap too! It turns out that they had all bought copies of the book for each other.

The grand total at the end of the day was six copies of the book given as presents, and endless laughter from all involved. After the flurry of gift giving was over with, they all spent a relaxing Christmas afternoon snuggled up under quilts reading their favorite stories of a little girl living on the prairie, occasionally chuckling at the funny coincidence that led to this memorable holiday.

materials

QUILT SIZE
73" x 81"

BLOCK SIZE
8" finished

SUPPLIES
1 package of 10" assorted green squares
3½ yards background fabric
¼ yard brown fabric
¼ yard yellow fabric

BORDER
1¼ yards

BINDING
¾ yard

BACKING
5 yards - vertical seam(s)

SAMPLE QUILT
Wilmington Essentials - Emerald Forest
10 Karat Gems for Wilmington Prints

1 cut

From the background fabric, cut:

- (4) 10" strips across the width of the fabric – subcut 3 strips into 10" squares and the remaining strip into (2) 10" squares for a **total of 14** squares.

- (9) 8½" strips across the width of the fabric – subcut the strips into the following increments:

  - 2 strips into (1) 8½" x 12½" rectangle and (1) 8½" x 28½" rectangle

  - 2 strips into (1) 8½" x 16½" rectangle and (1) 8½" x 24½" rectangle

  - 1 strip into (2) 8½" x 20½" rectangles

  - 2 strips into (1) 8½" x 28½" rectangle, (1) 8½" square, (1) 4½" x 8½" rectangle

  - 1 strip into (1) 8½" x 25" rectangle

  - Trim the remaining strip to 8½" x 40"

From the yellow fabric, cut:

- 1 star using the template found on page 13

From the brown fabric, cut:

- (1) 8½" square

2 make half-square triangles

On the reverse side of 14 background 10" squares, draw a line from corner to corner twice on the diagonal. **2A**

Select 14 assorted 10" green squares from the package. Layer a marked 10" background square with a green square with right sides facing. Sew on both sides of the drawn lines using a ¼" seam allowance. Cut the sewn squares in half vertically and horizontally. Then cut on the drawn lines. Open each section to reveal a half-square triangle unit. Each set of sewn squares will yield 8 half-square triangles for a **total of 112.** Press the seam allowance toward the darker fabric. Square up each half-square triangle to 4½". **2B**

2A

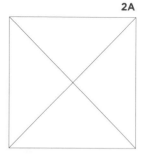

2B

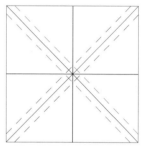

3A

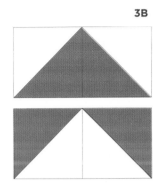

3B

3 block construction

Option 1 Pinwheels

Arrange 4 half-square triangles into a pinwheel as shown to complete 1 block. **3A**

Option 2 Chevrons

Sew 4 half-square triangle units into a 4-patch chevron as shown to complete 1 block. **3B**

Whichever option you choose, you will need a **total of 28** blocks.

Block Size: 8″ finished

4 arrange & sew

Note: the following instructions work for both option 1 and option 2 blocks.

Lay out the quilt in rows beginning at the bottom.

Row 1 - Sew a 28½″ background rectangle to either side of the brown square.

Row 2 – Sew 7 blocks together, then add a 4½″ background rectangle to either end.

Row 3 – Sew 6 blocks together, then add an 8½″ background square to either end.

Row 4 – Sew 5 blocks together, add a 12½″ rectangle to either end.

Row 5 – Sew 4 blocks together, add a 16½″ rectangle to either end.

Row 6 – Sew 3 blocks together, add a 20½″ rectangle to either end.

Row 7 – Sew 2 blocks together, add a 24½″ rectangle to either end.

Row 8 – Sew a 28½″ rectangle to either side of the remaining block.

Row 9 – Sew the 40″ strip and the 25″ rectangle together to make the top strip.

Sew the rows together.

To complete the center of the quilt, appliqué the star to the top row using a buttonhole stitch or a tiny zig zag.

5 border

Cut (8) 5″ strips across the width of the fabric. Sew the strips together end-to-end to make 1 long strip. Trim the borders from this strip.

Refer to Borders (pg. 110) in the Construction Basics to measure and cut the outer borders. The strips are approximately 72½″ for the sides and approximately 73½″ for the top and bottom.

6 quilt & bind

Layer the quilt with batting and backing and quilt. After the quilting is complete, square up the quilt and trim away all excess batting and backing. Add binding to complete the quilt. See the Construction Basics (pg. 110) for binding instructions.

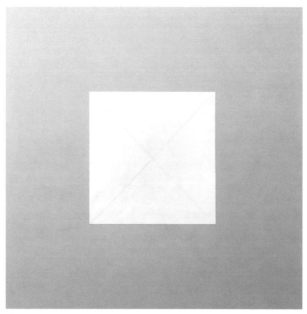

1 Mark both diagonal lines on the reverse side of a 10″ background square.

2 Lay the marked square on top of a 10″ green square with right sides facing. Sew on both sides of each marked line using a ¼″ seam allowance. Cut the square in half vertically and horizontally, and on both marked lines. Open to reveal 8 half-square triangles. Make 112 half-square triangles.

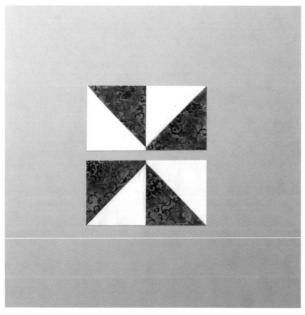

3 Arrange 4 half-square triangles in 2 rows of 2 to form a pinwheel block as shown. Sew the rows together and press in opposite directions. Make 28 pinwheel blocks.

4 If you wish to make chevron blocks instead of pinwheel blocks, arrange 4 half-square triangles in 2 rows of 2 as shown. Sew the rows together and press in opposite directions. Make 28 chevron blocks for option 2.

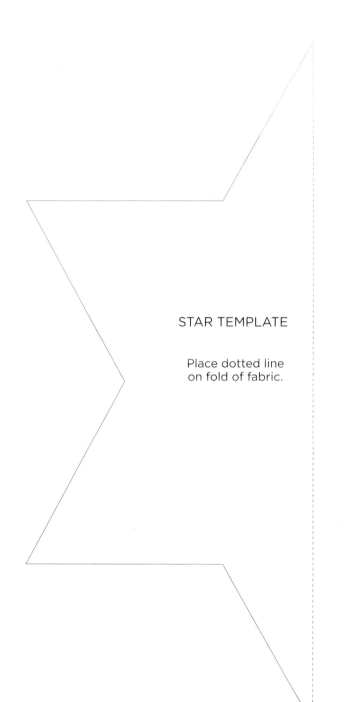

STAR TEMPLATE

Place dotted line
on fold of fabric.

disappearing hourglass crazy eight

Thanksgiving is one of my very favorite holidays for many reasons. Being surrounded by dear friends and loved ones is the best, and I enjoy each and every part of a Thanksgiving dinner, from the turkey and stuffing to the Jell-o salad and rolls. But, my very favorite part of Thanksgiving dinner is going around the table and saying what we are all grateful for. It's heartwarming to hear the sweet answers from my grandchildren and the thoughtful responses from my children now that they are grown. My heart is full to bursting when I think about how blessed we are.

My friend Paulene has a lovely Thanksgiving tradition that's similar to our own family tradition. In our family, we have a thankful turkey. I make a "naked" turkey out of construction paper and put a bowl of paper feathers close by where everyone can write what they are thankful for and help dress the turkey. In her family, they have a "Thankful Box."

Each year, Paulene carefully wraps a small box with brown paper and decorates it with her own personal design featuring hand cut fall leaves, a turkey, and the words, "I'm Thankful For" written on the side. It sits right in the center of her dining table with strips of paper next to it. The idea is that any time a member of her family feels so inclined, they fill out a strip of paper with what they are thankful for and drop it into the box. As the month goes by, the box fills up. Then, during Thanksgiving dinner, the box is emptied out and the little strips of paper are each read in turn by the entire family until the box is empty.

When her children were younger, the responses were a lot simpler. They generally said they were thankful for things like: "food, clothes, a house, my toys," and so on. But then, the responses started getting more insightful. As the years passed, they became more specific and might say things like: "I'm thankful for the kind person who found my keys at the movie theater." "I'm thankful for my good health." "I'm thankful that I can learn from my mistakes." "I'm thankful for challenges that help me to grow." Each year, when the table is cleared, Paulene gathers up these strips of paper and keeps them to reread whenever she needs a reminder of what is most important in life.

Even the smallest expression of gratitude can turn a day around. I've always believed, like Abraham Lincoln said, that "folks are usually about as happy as they make up their minds to be." And, from what I gather, happiness comes from recognizing the things we might take for granted. That's why Thanksgiving is so special. I love that it's a holiday about gratitude. And, of course, being grateful isn't just for one day a year; I try to write down a few things each day that I'm grateful for. I have a running list that I like to look back on often. What might be on your list?

For the tutorial and everything
you need to make this quilt visit
www.msqc.co/holidayblock19

materials

QUILT SIZE
82½" x 93¾"

BLOCK SIZE
11¼" finished

QUILT TOP
1 package 10" print squares
1 package 10" black squares

INNER BORDER
¾ yard

OUTER BORDER
1¾ yards

BINDING
¾ yard

BACKING
8½ yards - vertical seam(s)
or 3 yards of 108" wide

SAMPLE QUILT
Autumn Time by Color Principle for
Henry Glass

1 half-square triangles

Pair 1 print square with 1 black square with right sides facing. Sew all around the perimeter using a ¼" seam allowance. **1A**

Cut across the sewn square on both diagonals to make 4 half-square triangles. Press seams toward the black fabric. **1B**

Note: You may find a rotating or small cutting mat helpful for the making of this quilt. Simply make all the cuts in 1 direction, rotate the mat and make the remaining cuts. This reduces the chance of accidentally shifting the pieces between cuts and results in better accuracy.

Repeat with all remaining 10" squares to make 168 half-square triangles. Keep matching units stacked together.

2 hourglass blocks

Arrange 4 matching half-square triangle units in a 4-patch formation as shown to make an hourglass block. Sew into 2 rows and press the seams toward the darker triangle. Sew the 2 rows together to complete the block. **2A**
Make 42 blocks.

3 cut

Square up the hourglass block to 12¾". This will make cutting the block into thirds much easier. Be sure to trim this block symmetrically, so each edge of the block is 6⅜" from the center seam. Each of the 9 squares will measure 4¼". This measurement divided by 2 (=2⅛") will allow you to use the center seams as the cutting guides.

Cut the hourglass blocks into (9) 4¼" squares. Measure and cut 2⅛" away from the center seam on both sides, turning the block as needed without disturbing it. **3A**

4 swap, turn, & sew

The first and last pieces of the top row swap places and rotate so the corner points toward the center of the block. The first and last pieces of the bottom row swap places and rotate so the corner points toward the center of the block. **4A**

The 4-patch in the center of the middle row rotates 90°. The first and last pieces of the middle row rotate 180° so they point toward the center of the block. **4B**

1A

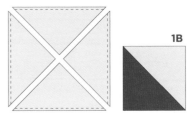

1B

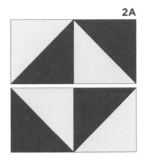

2A

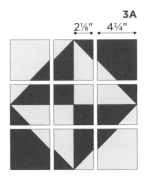

3A

2⅛" 4¼"

Sew the block together in rows. Press the seams of the first and last row towards the outside of the rows. Press the seams of the middle row toward the center of the row. Nest the seams and sew the rows together to complete the block. **4C** **Make 42** blocks.

Block Size: 11¼″ finished

5 arrange & sew

Lay out the blocks in rows. Each row is made up of **6 blocks** and **7 rows** are needed. After the blocks have been sewn into rows, press the seam allowances of the odd rows toward the right and the even rows toward the left to make the seams nest.

Sew the rows together to complete the center of the quilt.

6 inner border

Cut (8) 2½″ strips across the width of the black fabric. Sew the strips together end-to-end to make 1 long strip. Trim the borders from this strip.

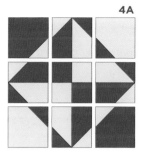

4A

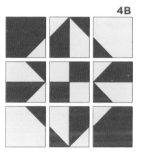

4B

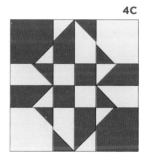

4C

Refer to Borders (pg. 110) in the Construction Basics to measure and cut the inner borders. The strips are approximately 79¼″ for the sides and approximately 72″ for the top and bottom.

7 outer border

From the outer border fabric, cut (9) 6″ strips across the width of the fabric. Sew the strips together end-to-end to make 1 long strip. Trim the borders from this strip.

Refer to Borders (pg. 110) in the Construction Basics to measure and cut the outer borders. The strips are approximately 83¼″ for the sides and 83″ for the top and bottom.

8 quilt & bind

Layer the quilt with batting and backing and quilt. After the quilting is complete, square up the quilt and trim away all excess batting and backing. Add binding to complete the quilt. See Construction Basics (pg. 110) for binding instructions.

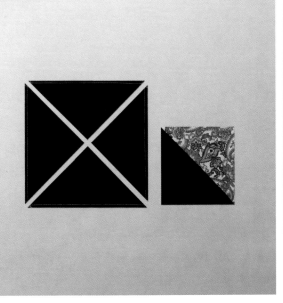

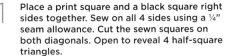

1 Place a print square and a black square right sides together. Sew on all 4 sides using a ¼" seam allowance. Cut the sewn squares on both diagonals. Open to reveal 4 half-square triangles.

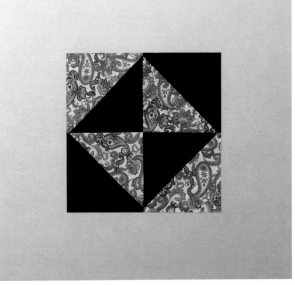

2 Arrange the 4 half-square triangles into a 4-patch formation as shown to make an hourglass block. Square the block up to 12¾". Be sure to trim it symmetrically, so each edge of the block is 6⅜" from the center seam.

3 Cut the hourglass block twice horizontally, 2⅛" on either side of the horizontal center seam. Cut the hourglass block twice vertically, 2⅛" on either side of the vertical center seam to yield 9 pieces.

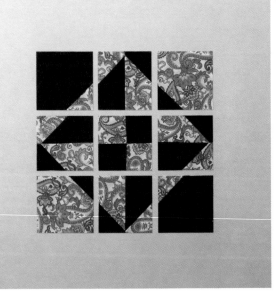

4 Swap the first and last pieces of the top row of the block. Repeat for the bottom row. Rotate the outer corner pieces so they point toward the block's center. Rotate the 4-patch in the center 90°.

5 Rotate the first and last pieces of the middle row 180° so they point toward the center of the block.

6 Sew the block together in rows. Press the first and last row toward the outside of the block and the middle row toward the center. Nest the seams and sew the rows together.

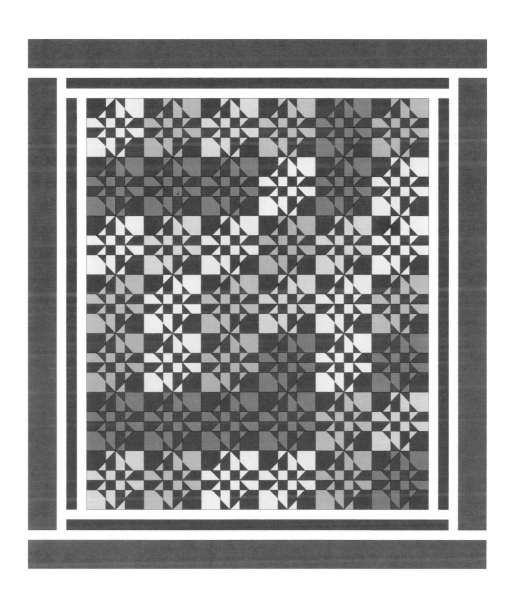

geese in motion

When does the Christmas season officially begin? When is it okay to deck the halls and bust out your favorite holiday tunes? For some of us, the merriment kicks off the day after Halloween; others put it off until Christmas Eve. For us quilters, we've got Christmas on the mind almost year-round as we stitch up holiday cheer for months in advance. But when it comes to the annual debut of the Christmas tree, folks can be pretty particular.

My friend Karen was the youngest of seven noisy, playful children. When she was a little girl, she could hardly wait for Christmastime. All December long, she begged her mother to put up the Christmas tree. All December, her mother put it off. And I don't blame her. Putting up the tree was a lot of work. It took up so much space and was more likely than not to be knocked over at some point by wrestling brothers. In short, it was a hassle Karen's mother did not relish.

Finally, on the very last Sunday before Christmas, Dad brought the tree up from the storage room and started detangling twinkle lights. He plugged in a string only to find a dozen or so burnt out lights. He hunted the garage for replacement bulbs. He worked and he worked for what seemed like hours. Karen was a bubbling mess of excitement and impatience.

"When I grow up," Karen silently vowed, "I'll put my tree up whenever I want!"

Years passed. Karen, now a young college student, was the only sibling left at home. It was Halloween night and everyone had come home for a Halloween dinner at Grandma's house. When the little nieces and nephews headed out to trick or treat, Karen offered to pass out

candy while her parents relaxed in the back family room. Then she went to work.

Ever so quietly she pulled the Christmas tree box up the basement steps. She peeked around the corner and saw her parents, totally oblivious to the mischief that was about to take place. When the kids returned with their bags full of candy, Karen held a finger to her lips and swore the children to secrecy.

At the end of the night, Karen's mother walked the kids to the front door to bid them farewell. Out of the corner of her eye she spied something twinkly. There, in the parlor was the Christmas tree, fully lit and dressed to the nines with shining ornaments, tinsel, and a smiling Christmas angel.

Karen came bursting into the hallway triumphantly. "Happy Halloween, Mother! Or should I say … Feliz Navidad!"

And so began the tradition of Karen's sneak-attack Christmas tree. Her parents celebrated their anniversary in March with a weekend in the city. They came home to a Christmas tree. On the Fourth of July, a "headache" kept Karen home from the firework show. Once again, her parents came home to a Christmas tree. And when Karen's parents moved to a neighboring state for a one-year volunteer assignment, Karen's tree stood proud and sparkling for a full twelve months!

Purists may protest, but Karen doesn't care. "Christmas trees make me happy! Why wait 'til December?"

For the tutorial and everything
you need to make this quilt visit:
www.msqc.co/holidayblock19

materials

QUILT SIZE
73" x 70½"

QUILT TOP
1 roll of 2½" print strips
2 yards background fabric
  – includes inner border

OUTER BORDER
1¼ yards

BINDING
¾ yard

BACKING
4½ yards – vertical seam(s)

OTHER
Binding Tool by TQM Products

SAMPLE QUILT
Holiday Lodge by Deb Strain
for Moda Fabrics

1 cut

Open the roll of print strips and leave each strip folded. Stack 2 to 4 strips atop each other and trim off the selvages. Align the blunt edge of the binding tool with the trimmed edge of the strips. Cut the angle through all layers. Turn the binding tool 180° and align the angled end with the cut edge and, again, cut through all layers. Open the remaining portion of each strip (the piece that is still folded). Layer the strips with wrong sides facing and align the blunt edge of the binding tool with the end of the strips. Cut the angle. **1A**

Separate the cut strips into stacks. Place all pieces that have the right side of the fabric facing up together. We'll call these A pieces for the sake of clarity. Place all the pieces that have the fabric facing down into another stack which we will call B pieces. Notice how the A pieces and B pieces are mirror images of each other. There will be a **total of 100** A pieces and **100** B pieces in each stack. **1B**

From the background fabric, cut:
- (25) 2½" strips across the width of the fabric – subcut 13 strips into 2½" squares.

1A

Each strip will yield 16 squares and a **total of 203** are needed. Cut 3 squares from corner to corner once on the diagonal to make 6 triangles. There will be 1 triangle and 5 squares left over for another project. Set aside the remaining 12 strips for the sashing strips and inner border.

- (1) 6¼" strip across the width of the fabric – subcut the strip into (3) 6¼" squares and (3) 5" squares. Cut each square once on the diagonal to make triangles.

1B

B   A

2 snowball the A & B pieces

On the reverse side of each 2½" square, draw a line from corner to corner once on the diagonal or fold the square once on the diagonal and press a crease in place to mark a sewing line. **2A**

2A

Place a marked square on the blunt end of each A and B piece. Make sure the right sides are facing and be aware of the orientation of the diagonal of the square when placed on the A pieces opposed to those placed on the B pieces. **2B**

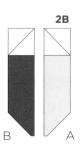

2B

B   A

2C

Sew on the marked line. Trim away the excess fabric ¼″ from the sewn seam. Press toward the outer edge of the strip. Stack all A pieces together and all B pieces together. **2C 2D**

3 build the horizontal rows

Select (1) 2½″ background triangle, 20 A pieces and 20 B pieces. Align the snowballed end of an A piece with 1 edge of the triangle with right sides facing. Sew the triangle in place as shown. Add a B piece to the other side of the triangle and stitch in place. See Diagram **3C**. Open and press. **3A 3B 3C**

Add an A piece, then a B piece. Continue alternating the A and B pieces until you have made a row using 20 A pieces and 20 B pieces. **3D**

Pick up a 5″ background triangle and sew it to the B side of the row with right sides facing. Open and press the seams toward the darker fabric. **3E 3F**

Stitch a 6¼″ triangle to the A side of the strip with right sides facing. Open and press the seam allowance toward the darker fabric. **3G 3H**

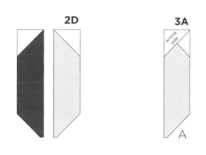

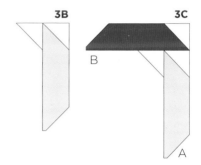

Square up the opposite end of the row by trimming it flush with the bottom of the triangle with which you began the row initially. **Make 5** rows. **3I**

4 make horizontal sashing

Pick up 9 of the 2½″ background strips you set aside earlier. Sew the strips together end-to-end to make 1 long strip. Cut the sashing rectangles from the strip. Each strip needs to be approximately 58½″ long and **6 strips** are needed. Refer to the diagram on page 29 and lay out the rows. Notice rows 2 and 4 are oriented differently than rows 1, 3, and 5. Sew a sashing strip between each pieced row. Add a sashing strip to the top and bottom as well.

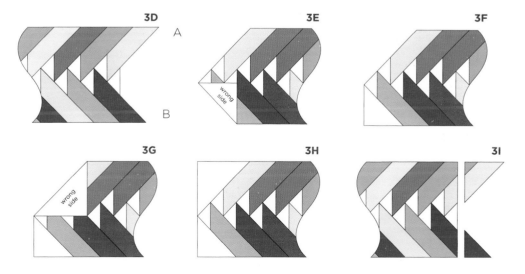

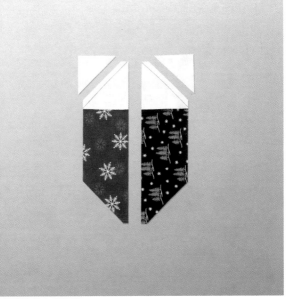

1 Place a marked background square on the blunt end of an A and B piece making sure the marked line is not parallel to the cut angle of the print piece. Sew on the marked line and trim away the excess fabric. Repeat with all remaining A and B pieces.

2 Press toward the background fabric.

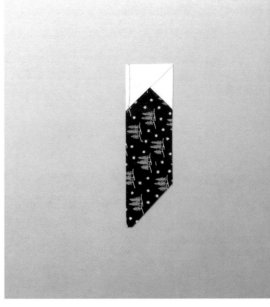

3 Place a 2½" background triangle right sides together with an A piece. Sew the pieces together along the edge of the triangle.

4 Press the triangle away from the A piece.

5 Add a B piece to the other side of the triangle and stitch in place. Open and press.

6 Continue adding on additional pieces until you have a total of 20 A pieces and 20 B pieces forming a row. Make 5 rows.

5 inner border

The inner border consists of a 2½"
background strip sewn to either side of
the sashed rows. Pick up the 3 remaining
strips that were set aside earlier. Sew the
3 strips together to make 1 long strip. Cut
the 2 side borders from this strip. Each
strip should measure approximately 60".
Sew 1 to the left side and 1 to the right.

6 outer border

Cut (7) 6" strips across the width of the
fabric. Sew the strips together end-to-end
to make 1 long strip. Trim the borders from
this strip.

Refer to Borders (pg. 110) in the
Construction Basics to measure and
cut the outer borders. The strips are
approximately 60" for the sides
and approximately 73½" for the top
and bottom.

7 quilt & bind

Layer the quilt with batting and backing
and quilt. After the quilting is complete,
square up the quilt and trim away all
excess batting and backing. Add binding
to complete the quilt. See Construction
Basics (pg. 110) for binding instructions.

spring twist

"Call me crazy, but I don't like Thanksgiving dinner." Everyone looked up from their notes and stared at Camille, one of our writers here at Missouri Star. "Don't get me wrong, I love spending time with family—and giving thanks is lovely—I just wish the food was different. How about a Thanksgiving taco bar? Or a pizza shaped like a turkey?"

Her comment got me thinking about all the traditions of Thanksgiving dinner, so I decided to do a bit of research.

Every year on the fourth Thursday of November, American families and friends gather around the dinner table for a Thanksgiving feast. And what's being served? The same exact dishes! Whether you live in a Manhattan high-rise or a quaint country farmhouse, chances are your dinner looks a lot like this: Roast turkey, stuffing, mashed potatoes, cranberry sauce, and pumpkin pie. Why do we all eat the same foods? It's tradition, of course! But is it historically accurate? Well ... not really.

Records show that in 1621, a group of Pilgrims and Wampanoag Indians in Plymouth celebrated the harvest with a giant feast. Storybook depictions of the first Thanksgiving show a cheerful crowd seated at long tables filled with all the traditional staples. The trouble is, that 17th century feast didn't look a thing like your Thanksgiving dinner.

Did they really eat turkey? Maybe. But maybe not. There's actually no proof either way!

Mashed potatoes? Nope. Potatoes had not yet been introduced to North America. (Tragic, I know.)

Cranberry sauce? Zip! Cranberry sauce didn't become a "thing" for another fifty years.

Surely there was pumpkin pie? Sorry, no. With no butter or flour for crust, pumpkin pie was nowhere to be found. (Same story for fresh-baked dinner rolls. Sigh.)

Believe it or not, if you want your Thanksgiving feast to be truly authentic, get ready to dine on venison, seafood, freshly harvested vegetables, and, perhaps, a bit of turkey.

But in my opinion, it doesn't really matter what you eat. The real heart of Thanksgiving isn't what is on the menu, it's the folks sitting around the table. We gather together to focus on life's many blessings. That, to me, is the very essence of Thanksgiving—whether we're feasting on turkey, lasagna, or peanut butter sandwiches. But as for me and my house, I think we'll stick with turkey!

For the tutorial and everything
you need to make this quilt visit:
www.msqc.co/holidayblock19

materials

QUILT SIZE
63" x 69"

BLOCK SIZE
6" finished

QUILT TOP
1 roll 2½" print strips
1¼ yards complementary fabric
  - includes inner border

OUTER BORDER
1¼ yards

BINDING
¾ yard

BACKING
4¼ yards – vertical seam(s)

SAMPLE QUILT
Artisan Batiks Cornucopia 10
by Lunn Studios for Robert Kaufman

1 cut

From the roll of 2½" strips, select 36 strips. Cut each strip into 6½" rectangles. Each strip will yield 6 and a **total of 216** rectangles are needed.

From the complementary fabric, cut:

- (15) 2½" strips across the width of the fabric – subcut 9 strips into 2½" squares. Each strip will yield 16 squares and a **total of 144** are needed. Set aside the remaining 6 strips for the inner border.

2 snowball rectangles

Mark a line from corner to corner once on the diagonal on the reverse side of the 2½" squares. Place a square atop a rectangle with right sides facing. Sew on the marked line. Trim the excess fabric away ¼" from the sewn seam. **Make 144** units. **2A**

3 block construction

Select 2 snowballed units and a 2½" x 6½" rectangle. Sew the 3 pieces together as shown to complete 1 block. Notice the widest part of the snowballed unit touches the inner rectangle. **Make 72. 3A**

Block Size: 6" finished

4 arrange & sew

Lay out the blocks in rows. Each row is made up of **8 blocks** and **9 rows** are needed. As you lay out the blocks, notice how each block is oriented. Refer to the diagram on page 37. After the blocks have been sewn into rows, press the seam allowances of the odd-numbered rows toward the right and the even-numbered rows toward the left to make the seams nest.

Sew the rows together to complete the center of the quilt.

2A

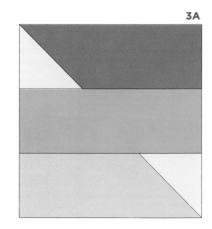

3A

5 inner border

Pick up the (6) 2½" strips that were set aside. Sew the strips together end-to-end to make 1 long strip. Trim the borders from this strip.

Refer to Borders (pg. 110) in the Construction Basics to measure and cut the inner borders. The strips are approximately 54½" for the sides and approximately 52½" for the top and bottom.

6 outer border

Cut (6) 6" strips across the width of the fabric. Sew the strips together end-to-end to make 1 long strip. Trim the borders from this strip.

Refer to Borders (pg. 110) in the Construction Basics to measure and cut the outer borders. The strips are approximately 58½" for the sides and approximately 63½" for the top and bottom.

7 quilt & bind

Layer the quilt with batting and backing and quilt. After the quilting is complete, square up the quilt and trim away all excess batting and backing. Add binding to complete the quilt. See Construction Basics (pg. 110) for binding instructions.

spring twist quilt

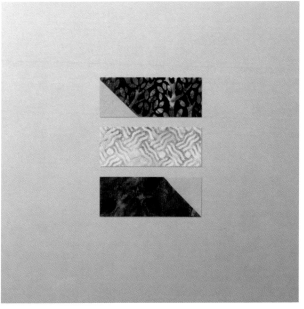

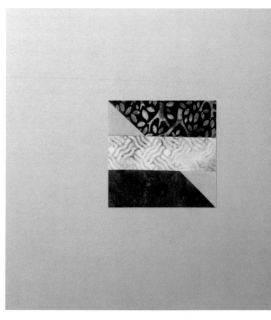

1 Mark a diagonal line on the reverse side of a 2½" complementary square. Place the marked square on top of a 2½" x 6½" rectangle with right sides facing making note of the orientation of the marked line. Sew on the marked line and trim away the excess fabric. Press toward the snowballed corner. Make 144 snowballed rectangles.

2 Select 2 snowballed rectangles and a 2½" x 6½" rectangle. Arrange them as shown.

3 Sew the 2 snowballed rectangles to the long sides of the 2½" x 6½" rectangle to complete the block. Make 72.

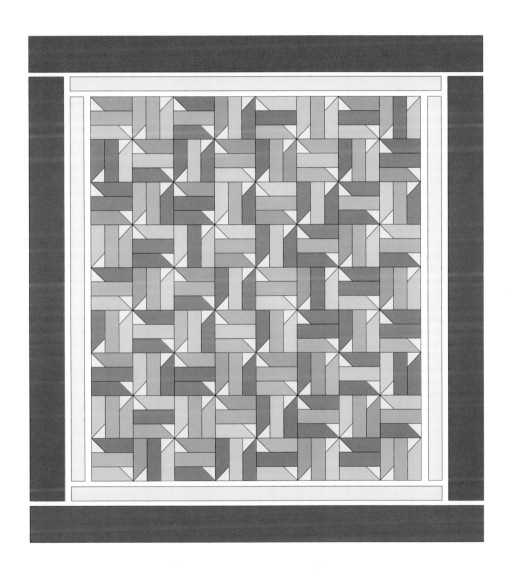

For the tutorial and everything you need to make this quilt visit: **www.msqc.co/holidayblock19**

diamond pavers

Halloween was always a special holiday for Jennifer and her daughter, Julie. All October long, their home would be decorated with spooktacular orange lights, fuzzy fake cobwebs, and grinning jack-o-lanterns. Jennifer would also make sure she had the best batch of candy for all the kids! Every Halloween night, there would be a line of trick-or-treaters anxiously awaiting their turn to get a king-sized candy bar. But what Jennifer loved most about Halloween was playing a trick or two! Usually, she would have Julie hide somewhere in their yard and sneak up on unsuspecting visitors, but this year she wanted to try something a little different.

Leaving Julie on candy duty, Jennifer went to the little storage closet beneath the stairs and pulled out a big tote box. Stuffed inside were some of Julie's past Halloween costumes, one of which included a long black cloak. "Oh, this is perfect!" Jennifer said as she held the cloak up. "Julie, come here!"

Julie followed her mom's voice into the hallway, "What is it, Mom?" When she saw the long black cloak her mom was holding, she knew this year's trick would be one to remember! Jennifer painted Julie's face ghostly white, dabbed dark eyeshadow around her eyes to give her a ghoulish look, and then she had her put on the cloak with the hood pulled down over her head.

Jennifer looked outside to make sure no trick-or-treaters were on the porch. "Okay," she said as she opened the door, "the coast is clear, now stand right out here in the corner and pretend you're a statue."

Julie stood by the door and waited. A few minutes went by before a trick-or-treater approached the porch. She carefully peeked to see who was coming. This trick-or-treater was particularly tall and his costume was nothing more than a huge pumpkin where his head was supposed to be. Trying hard not to giggle, Julie kept her head down as the pumpkin head approached. Jennifer opened the door with the candy bowl tucked under her arm, also stifling a laugh. Holding his massive orange head aloft with one hand and his candy bag out with the other, the pumpkin head cautiously walked past Julie towards Jennifer. "Trick or ..."

"BOO!" Julie yelled as she sprung to life. The pumpkin head let out a muffled shriek and bolted towards the end of the porch, but his head became entangled in the cobwebs hanging above! Still shrieking, the trick-or-treater tried yanking the pumpkin off his head to free himself from the sticky cobwebs.

"Oh goodness, calm down!" Jennifer chuckled as she went to help untangle him from the fake webs.

"Wow," the pumpkin head said, "people usually give me candy when I say 'trick-or-treat'!"

"Who said you weren't getting any treats?" For being such a good sport, Jennifer and Julie let the pumpkin-headed trick-or-treater take two king-sized candy bars from the bowl, and wished him a Happy Halloween.

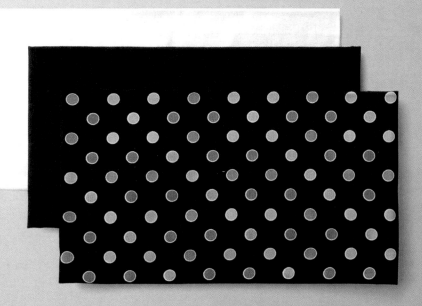

materials

QUILT SIZE
68" x 68"

BLOCK SIZE
9½" finished

QUILT TOP
1 package 10" print squares
1½ yards white fabric
1½ yards black fabric

BORDER
1¼ yards

BINDING
¾ yard

BACKING
4¼ yards – vertical seam(s)

SAMPLE QUILT
Ghostly Glow Town by Shelly Comiskey
for Henry Glass

1 cut

From the white fabric, cut:

- (5) 10½″ strips across the width of the fabric. Subcut 4 strips vertically into (16) 2½″ x 10½″ rectangles. Subcut the remaining strip vertically into (8) 2½″ x 10½″ rectangles. Set aside the remainder of the strip for another project. You will have a **total of 72** rectangles.

From the black fabric, cut:

- (5) 10½″ strips across the width of the fabric. Subcut 4 strips vertically into (16) 2½″ x 10½″ rectangles. Subcut the remaining strip vertically into (8) 2½″ x 10½″ rectangles. Set aside the remainder of the strip for another project. You will have a **total of 72** rectangles.

2 select & sort

Select 36 contrasting 10″ print squares from the package. Sort them into 2 stacks, 1 of lights and 1 of darks.

3 block construction

Place a 2½″ x 10½″ white rectangle on top of a dark 10″ square with right sides facing. The rectangle needs to be angled approximately 2″ in from the edge of the square at the top and at least ¼″ in from the bottom edge. Sew the rectangle in place using a ¼″ seam allowance. Press the strip over the seam allowance toward the outer edge of the square. Repeat for the adjacent side of the square. **3A 3B 3C 3D**

Turn the square over so the wrong side is facing up. Using the square as a guide, trim off the excess fabric showing beyond the edges. **3E 3F**

Flip the square back over with the right side facing up. Add a white rectangle to the two remaining sides of the square using the same process as before. Notice how the wider portions of the rectangles cross over each other. **3G**

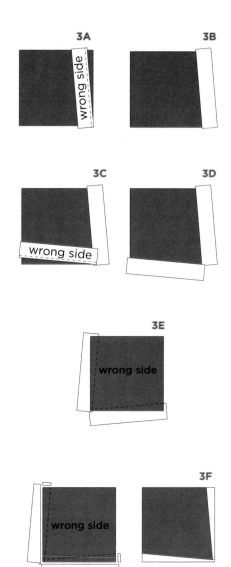

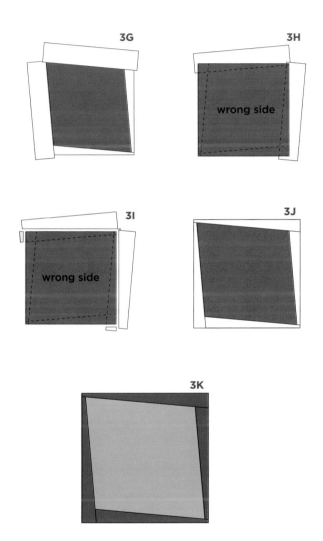

3G

3H

wrong side

3I

wrong side

3J

3K

Again, turn the reverse side of the square up. Trim as before to complete the block. **Make 18** blocks using the white rectangles and dark print squares. **3H 3I 3J**

Repeat the instructions for adding rectangles to the squares using the black rectangles with the light squares. **Make 18. 3K**

Block Size: 9½" finished

4 arrange & sew

Lay out the blocks in rows, alternating the blocks framed with white rectangles with those framed with black rectangles. Refer to the diagram on page 45. Each row is made up of **6 blocks** and **6 rows** are needed.

5 border

Cut (7) 6" strips across the width of the fabric. Sew the strips together end-to-end to make 1 long strip. Trim the borders from this strip.

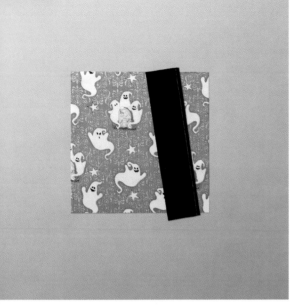

1   Place a black rectangle atop a light print square with right sides facing. The rectangle needs to be angled approximately 2″ in from the edge of the square at the top and at least ¼″ in from the bottom edge. Sew in place using a ¼″ seam allowance.

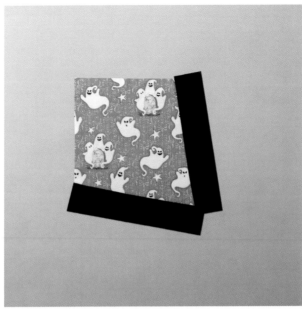

2   Press the rectangle to cover the edge of the square and repeat the process to add a second black rectangle to the adjacent side of the square. Be sure to angle the second rectangle so the smaller margins of both rectangles cross in the same corner of the square and the wider margins are on opposite corners.

3   Turn the square over so the wrong side is facing up. Trim off the excess fabric showing beyond the edges of the square.

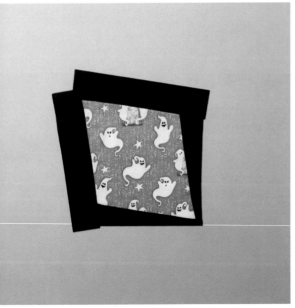

4   Flip the square back over and repeat the same process to add the 2 additional black rectangles to the remaining sides of the square. Be sure the wider portions of the rectangles cross over each other.

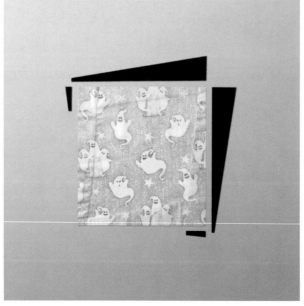

5   Turn the square back over so the wrong side is facing up again. Use the square to trim off the excess fabric.

6   Make 18 blocks using light print squares and black rectangles.

Refer to Borders (pg. 110) in the Construction Basics to measure and cut the outer borders. The strips are approximately 57½" for the sides and approximately 68½" for the top and bottom.

6 quilt & bind

Layer the quilt with batting and backing and quilt. After the quilting is complete, square up the quilt and trim away all excess batting and backing. Add binding to complete the quilt. See Construction Basics (pg. 110) for binding instructions.

For the tutorial and everything you need to make this quilt visit:
www.msqc.co/holidayblock19

jenny's winter wall hanging

Fresh-cut or artificial, elegant or homey, the Christmas tree is the centerpiece of our holiday celebrations.

Some are decked out in red and green with traditional tinsel and twinkle lights. Some are like a travel log, with ornaments gathered from across the globe. Some are expensive and fragile; some are adorned with kid-made decorations constructed out of paper, popsicle sticks, and glitter. No matter the style, my favorite trees are always the ones dressed from trunk to star in memories.

Missouri Star's own Stephany Beaver puts up four artificial beauties ranging in height from six to seventeen feet, all covered in sentimental ornaments. Years and years ago, Stephany's great grandfather started the annual tradition of giving meaningful ornaments to his loved ones. Now that Stephany is grown, she continues that tradition with her own family.

Every year as Christmas draws near, Stephany picks out a new ornament for each member of the family. She always chooses something special to commemorate highlights from the year. One year the family started raising chickens, so, of course, they needed a chicken ornament. And the year the Kansas City Royals took home the pennant, a Royals ornament was added to the collection.

After Stephany's son started playing basketball, he received a miniature replica of his #22 jersey. Stephany's first professional speaking engagement was commemorated with a cute little microphone ornament. And when Stephany's stepdaughter went to work for Disney, she was given a Cinderella ornament. (That same stepdaughter has a Miss Kansas Teen USA ornament from 2013 when she won the title!) Stephany's husband was given a Charlie Brown kite ornament because he always gets his kites stuck in trees, and he's a bit of a Charlie Brown look-alike, too!

I can only imagine how fun it must be to pull out the Christmas boxes and decorate the tree every year. Each ornament carries so many memories, and together they are like a family scrapbook of years gone by. Stephany says that when the kids are grown, they will each take their collection of ornaments to decorate their own trees, and hopefully the tradition will be carried on for generations to come!

materials

SIZE
48" x 42"

PROJECT TOP
1 package 10" print squares
1½ yards background fabric
   - includes inner border
¼ yard cuddle fabric

OUTER BORDER
¾ yards

BINDING
¾ yard

BACKING
3 yards - vertical seam(s)

OTHER
2 large buttons
Missouri Star Quilt Co.
   - Large Simple Wedge Template
   - Large Half-Hexagon Template

SAMPLE PROJECT
The Joy of Giving by Susan Winget for
Wilmington Prints

1 stars

Select (4) 10″ print squares. From each, cut (2) 2½″ strips across – subcut into 2½″ squares. Each strip yields 4 squares and 5 squares are needed from each for a **total of (20)** 2½″ print squares.

Cut (3) 2½″ strips across the width of the background fabric – subcut 2 strips into 2½″ squares. Each strip will yield 16 squares and a **total of 32** are needed. From the remaining strip, cut (4) 2½″ x 6½″ rectangles and (1) 2½″ x 8½″ rectangle.

Place a 2½″ print square on an angle (any angle) atop a 2½″ background square with right sides together. Sew ¼″ in from the angled edge of the print square. Trim ¼″ away from the sewn seam. **1A**

Press the piece flat, turn the square over and press the print piece over the seam allowance. Trim the edges evenly with the background square. (Set the trimmed scrap aside to make at least 2 star legs from each print square.) **1B**

Use the scrap from the first leg of the star to make another leg on the opposite side of the square. Make sure the second leg crosses over the first by at least ¼″. Stitch and trim as before. **1C 1D**

Repeat to make 4 sets of 4 matching star leg units from each print for a **total of 16** star leg units.

Gather (4) 2½″ background squares, 4 matching star leg units, and (1) 2½″ matching print square. Arrange the pieces to form a 9-patch block and sew together.

Sew (1) 2½″ x 6½″ background rectangle to one side of the star to complete the Star Block. **Make 4** Star Blocks. **1E**

Block Size: 6″ x 8″ finished

Sew 4 Star Blocks together in a row. Press to one direction. Sew (1) 2½″ x 8½″ background rectangle to the right side of the row. Press toward the background rectangle. Set aside until you are ready to assemble the quilt top. **1F**

Section Size: 26″ x 8″ finished

2 gnomes

Select (4) 10″ print squares, 2 for the gnome bodies and 2 for their hats.

Cut 2 wedges from (2) 10″ print squares using the Large Simple Wedge Template.

Cut 2 half-hexagons from each of (2) 10″ print squares for a **total of 4.**

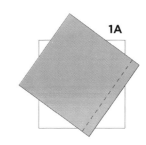

1A

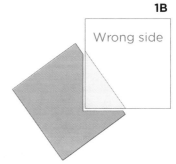

1B

Wrong side

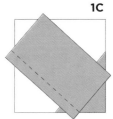

1C

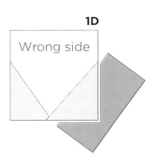

1D

Wrong side

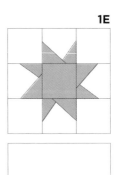

1E

Cut (1) 4¾" strip across the width of the background fabric. Subcut 4 half-hexagons from the strip using the template. Cut each half-hexagon in half for a **total of 8.**

Cut (1) 10" strip across the width of the background fabric. Subcut the strip into (2) 10" x 16" rectangles.

Fold the (2) 10" x 16" rectangles in half. Align the template as shown in. **2A**

Cut along the right edge. Open the fabric, reposition the template, and continue cutting the right side of the wedge across the remainder of the fabric. **2B**

Repeat to cut a wedge from the second rectangle.

Sew the print wedge to the left portion of the background rectangle, matching the bottom edge. Press toward the print fabric. Lay a ruler along the right edge of the print wedge and trim the right side of the background fabric even with the print wedge.

Sew the right background rectangle to the pieced unit to make the Gnome's hat. Press toward the background fabric. Trim this unit to 13½" x 9½". **2C**

Repeat to **make 2** Gnome Hat units.

Sew 2 halves of half-hexagons to the angled sides of each print half-hexagon.

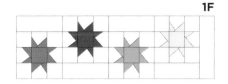
1F

Fold of fabric

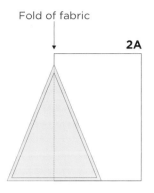
2A

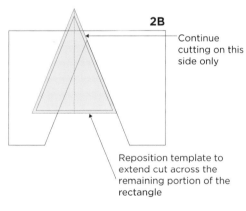
2B

Continue cutting on this side only

Reposition template to extend cut across the remaining portion of the rectangle

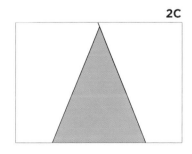
2C

2D

Press toward the background fabric. **Make 4** units. **2D**

Sew the matching, pieced half-hexagon units together to create the Gnome's Body. Press the seam in either direction. Trim the unit to 13½" x 8½" if necessary. Repeat to make a **total of 2** Gnome Body units. **2E**

Sew 1 Gnome Hat unit to the top of 1 Gnome Body unit. Press toward the Gnome Body unit. Repeat to make a **total of 2** Gnome Blocks.

Block Size: 13" x 17" finished

Sew 2 Gnome Blocks together and press to either side. Set aside until you are ready to assemble the quilt top. **2F**

Section Size: 26" x 17" finished

Note: The beards for the gnomes are added after the wall hanging has been quilted. See page 55 for instructions.

Option: If you don't like the fluffiness of our cuddly beards, you could substitute a quilting cotton fabric and appliqué the beard onto your quilt top before or after quilting.

3 gifts

Select (4) 10" print squares. From each 10" square, cut:

- (1) 2½" strip across the square – Subcut (4) 2½" squares from each print.

- (2) 1½" strips across the square – Subcut (1) 1½" x 5½" rectangle, (2) 1½" x 2½" rectangles, and (2) 1½" squares from each print. **3A**

From the background fabric, cut:

- (1) 1½" strip across the width of the fabric – Subcut (4) 1½" x 3" rectangles and (8) 1½" x 1¾" rectangles.

- (2) 2½" strips across the width of the fabric – Subcut (1) 2½" x 26½" rectangle and (3) 2½" x 6½" rectangles for sashing.

Select 4 matching 2½" print squares. Pair the squares with (1) 1½" x 5½" rectangle and (2) 1½" x 2½" rectangles of a contrasting print fabric.

Sew a 2½" square to either side of a 1½" x 2½" rectangle. **Make 2** units. Press toward the rectangle. Sew a unit to either side of a 1½" x 5½" rectangle. Press toward the rectangle. Repeat to **make 4** Gift Box units. **3B**

On the wrong side of each 1½" print square, draw a line once on the diagonal from corner to corner. Place a marked 1½" print square on the left side of a 1½" x 3" background rectangle with right sides facing. Sew along the drawn line, trim the excess fabric away ¼" from the

2E

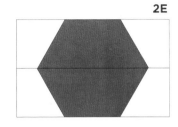

2F

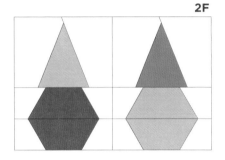

3A

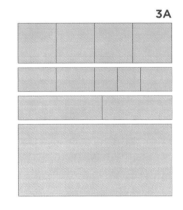

3B

sewn seam. Open and press. Repeat for the right side of the rectangle. Sew (1) 1½" x 1¾" rectangle of background fabric to the left and right sides of each these units. Repeat to **make 4** Bow units. **3C**

Sew 1 Bow unit to the top of the Gift Box unit that has the same print fabric for the ribbon. Press toward the Gift Box unit. **Make 4** Gift Blocks. **3D**

Block Size: 5" x 6" finished

Sew the Gift Blocks together in a row separated by 2½" x 6½" sashing. Press toward the sashing. Sew the 2½" x 26½" sashing strip to the top of the unit and press toward the sashing. Set aside until you are ready to assemble the quilt top. **3E**

Section Size: 26" x 8" finished

4 tree

Select 3-4 green 10" print squares to make the tree body and 1 brown 10" print square for the tree trunk. From each green square, cut (2) 5" x 10" rectangles. From 5 of these rectangles, cut 5 half-hexagons using the template. Trim 1 rectangle to 5" x 8½".

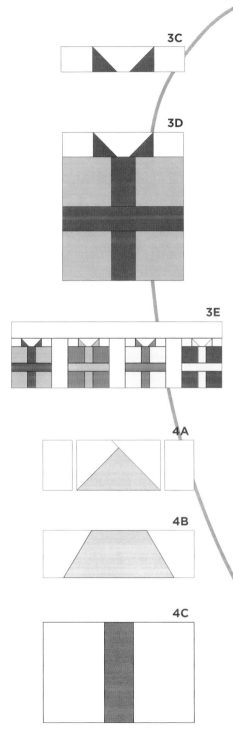

3C

3D

3E

4A

4B

4C

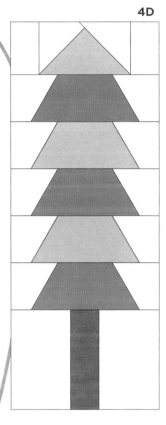

4D

Cut (1) 3″ x 9½″ rectangle from the brown print square for the tree trunk.

Cut (2) 4¾″ strips across the width of the background fabric – cut half-hexagons from the strip using the template. Each strip will yield 4 half-hexagons and 5 are needed. Set the extras aside for another project. Cut each of the 5 half-hexagons in half for a **total of 10.**

Cut (1) 5¾″ strip across the width of the background fabric. Subcut (2) 9½″ x 5¾″ rectangles.

Trim the remaining strip to 5″ wide. Subcut (2) 3″ x 5″ rectangles and (2) 5″ squares.

Place (1) 5″ background square on the left side of the 5″ x 8½″ rectangle of green print with right sides facing. Sew from the top right to bottom left of the square. Trim ¼″ away from seam and press toward the triangle. Repeat for the other side, sewing from the top left to the bottom right of the square. Trim ¼″ away from the seam and press toward the triangle. Sew (1) 3″ x 5″ rectangle of background fabric to the left and right sides of this unit. **4A**

Sew 2 halves of half-hexagons to the angled sides of each of the green print half-hexagon. Press toward the background fabric. Trim unit to 13½″ wide. **Make 5** half-hexagon units. **4B**

Sew the (2) 9½″ x 5¾″ rectangles to either side of the 3″ x 9½″ print rectangle. Press toward the center rectangle to make the trunk unit. **4C**

Sew the flying geese unit, the 5 pieced half-hexagon units, and the trunk unit together in a column in that order. Press toward the trunk. **4D**

Trim block to 13½″ x 33½″ if necessary. Set aside until you are ready to assemble the quilt top.
Block Size: 13″ x 33″ finished

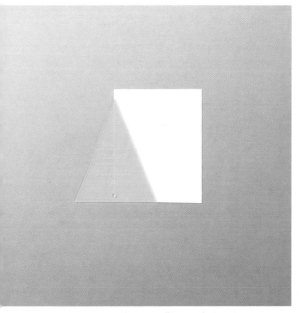

1 Fold a 10" x 16" background rectangle in half. Place the centerline of the template on top of the fold with the short side of the template even with the bottom of the fabric. Cut along the edge of the template to remove a wedge shape from the triangle.

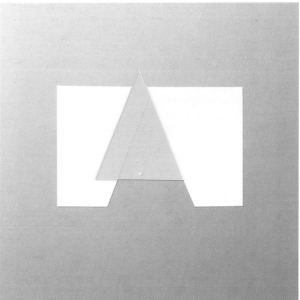

2 Unfold the fabric and lay the template on top matching the right edge of the ruler with the right edge of the wedge you just cut from the rectangle. Make sure the template extends past the top of the fabric and continue cutting along the right edge of the template to yield 2 separate pieces from the rectangle.

3 Sew a print wedge to the left portion of the background rectangle. Press toward the print wedge. Trim any excess background fabric even with the print wedge.

4 Sew the right portion of the background rectangle to the right edge of the print wedge. Press to complete a gnome hat.

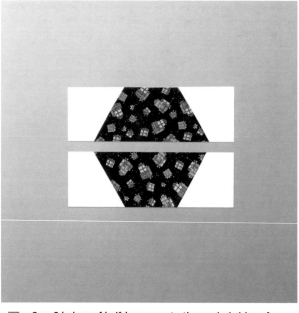

5 Sew 2 halves of half-hexagons to the angled sides of 2 matching half-hexagons. Press. Sew the 2 matching units together with the long sides of the half-hexagons touching. Press to complete a gnome body.

6 Sew a gnome hat to the top of a gnome body. Press toward the gnome body to complete the block.

5 arrange & sew

Sew the Stars to the top of the Gnomes. Add the Gifts to the bottom. Sew the Tree Block to the right side. Refer to the diagram below if necessary.

6 borders

Cut (2) 2½" strips across the width of the background fabric. Trim the strips for the inner border from these. Note: The inner border is only on the bottom and left side of the quilt.

Cut (5) 4" strips across the width of the border fabric. Sew the strips together end-to-end to make one long strip. Trim the strips for the outer border from these.

Always measure the quilt top 3 times before cutting borders. Start measuring about 4" in from each side and through the center horizontally. Take the average of those 3 measurements to determine the border length. The strips for the inner border are approximately 39½" for the bottom and 35½" for the left side. The outer borders are approximately 41½" for the top and bottom and the 42½" for the side outer borders.

Attach the bottom inner border first and the left inner border second. Position the border fabric on top as you sew. Having the border on top will prevent waviness and keep the quilt straight. Repeat this process to attach the outer borders, measuring the quilt 3 times before cutting. Include the newly attached borders in your measurements. Press toward the borders.

7 quilt & bind

Layer the quilt with batting and backing and quilt. After the quilting is complete, square up the quilt and trim away all excess batting and backing. Add binding to complete the quilt. See Construction Basics (pg. 110) for binding instructions.

8 adding the beards

Cut 2 beards from cuddle fabric following the templates on page 53 and 55. Choose a large button to make a nose for your gnome and sew the button to the quilt to attach the beard.

Tip: Use a Shop-Vac along the edges of the beard after you cut it to remove any excess fluffiness.

For the tutorial and everything
you need to make this quilt visit:
www.msqc.co/holidayblock19

brick yard

Any time you see a nice family portrait, take a moment of silence to recognize the blood, sweat, and tears that went into making that photo possible. Because behind those Kodak smiles, there's a good chance that little Sally spilled egg salad down the front of her dress and had to be changed last minute, and Ted re-combed his hair into spikes when no one was looking, and someone forgot to put shoes on the baby, and Mom is feeling like a flustered, sweaty mess! From planning outfits to wrangling wiggly kids, a trip to the portrait studio is no walk in the park!

I've had my fair share of behind-the-scenes chaos, but in chatting with a friend who used to develop film for a living, I heard a few tales that trump my most hectic photo shoots!

"One day, I was printing a set of photographs from a wedding. They had been taken on the grounds of the beautiful Salt Lake City temple, an elegant gothic-style building with exquisite details and extensive gardens.

In the first photo, the groom, bride, and her parents were carefully positioned in front of a large decorative pond with a smooth, glassy surface. The spires of the temple were reflected in the water alongside a brilliant blue sky and a fluffy cloud or two. Just lovely.

In the next picture, the bride's veil had become a bit unruly in the wind. The father of the bride seemed to be grabbing at its wild wispy layers while still maintaining a careful smile for the photo.

The third picture revealed a veil-less bride. Her face was a mixture of shock and horror. I scanned the background and gasped when I spotted that delicate veil floating on the surface of the pond water.

The fourth photo featured a man seated on a bench. I guessed him to be the best man or perhaps the brother of the bride. His socks and shoes had been removed and he was rolling up the legs of his black tuxedo. The fifth photo was snapped right as Mr. Save-the-Day took his first step into the water. But by this time, the veil had floated some fifteen feet away.

In the sixth photo, the man stood in the center of the pond, holding the dripping veil triumphantly over his head. I noticed one of his pant legs had slipped below his knee into the water. I flipped to the next photo to find out what happened next.

The seventh photo was exactly like the first: Bride, groom, mother, father, all standing in front of the pond with smiles on their faces. It was a beautiful photo—definitely frame worthy. But if I looked closely, I could see a few telltale droplets of water hanging from the edge of the veil. They say a picture is worth a thousand words; this one told a whole tale! But all in all, it seems, 'They lived happily ever after!'

materials

QUILT SIZE
64½ x 72¾"

BLOCK SIZE
8¼" finished

QUILT TOP
1 roll 2½" print strips
1 roll 2½" background strips
 – includes inner border

OUTER BORDER
1¼ yards

BINDING
¾ yard

BACKING
4½ yards – vertical seam(s)
 or 2¼ yards of 108" wide

SAMPLE QUILT
Holiday Flourish 12 by Peggy Toole for Robert
Kaufman Fabrics

1 cut

Select 6 background strips and set the rest aside for the moment. From 5 of the selected strips, cut (16) 2½" squares. Cut 4 additional 2½" squares from the sixth strip for a **total of 84** squares.

2 sew

Select 2 print strips and 1 background strip. Sew a print strip to each long side of the background strip. **2A**

Repeat to make 18 strip sets. Set 6 background strips aside for the inner border. Set the remaining background and print strips aside for another project.

Select 2 strip sets and lay them right sides together. Sew them together along both long sides to create a tube. **2B**

Repeat to **make 9** tubes.

3 cut

Pick up a ruler with a 45° marking. Align the 45° mark on your ruler with a seam line and cut. Slide or rotate the ruler as necessary to match the 45° mark on the ruler to the seam line again. **3A**

Match the ruler with the top of the last cut you made. Cut along the ruler's edge to make a triangle. Slide or rotate the ruler as necessary to continue cutting triangles from each tube. Each tube will yield 5 triangles and a **total of 42** are needed. **3B**

Open and press each unit toward the darker fabric. **3C**

Block Size: 8¼" finished

4 snowball the corners

Mark a diagonal line on the reverse side of each 2½" background square. Lay a marked square on a corner of the block as shown. Sew across the marked line. Trim ¼" away from the sewn seam to remove the excess fabric. **4A**

2A

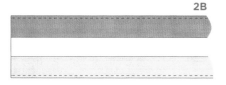

2B

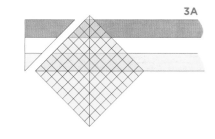

3A

3B

3C

Repeat for opposite corner of block. **4B**

Snowball the same 2 corners of the remaining blocks.

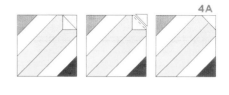

5 arrange & sew

Lay out the blocks in rows, making note of the orientation of the blocks in the diagram on page 63. Each row is made up of **6 blocks** and **7 rows** are needed. After the blocks have been sewn into rows, press the seam allowances of the odd rows toward the right and the even rows toward the left to make the seams nest.

Sew the rows together to complete the quilt top.

6 inner border

Pick up the (6) 2½" strips you set aside earlier. Sew the strips together end-to-end to make 1 long strip. Trim the border from this strip.

Refer to Borders (pg. 110) in the Construction Basics to measure and cut the inner borders. The strips are approximately 58¼" for the sides and 54" for the top and bottom.

7 outer borders

From the border fabric, cut (7) 6" strips across the width of the fabric. Sew the strips together end-to-end to make 1 long strip. Trim the borders from this strip.

Refer to Borders (pg. 110) in the Construction Basics to measure and cut the outer borders. The strips are approximately 62¼" for the sides and 65" for the top and bottom.

8 quilt & bind

Layer the quilt with batting and backing and quilt. After the quilting is complete, square up the quilt and trim away all excess batting and backing. Add binding to complete the quilt. See Construction Basics (pg. 110) for binding instructions.

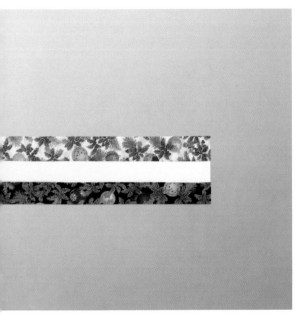

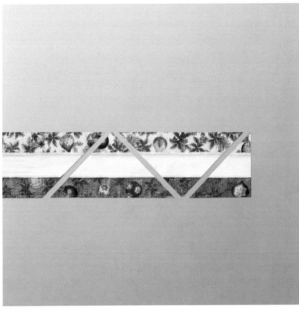

1 Sew a print strip to either long side of a background strip. Repeat to make 18 strip sets.

2 Sew 2 strip sets together to create a tube. Cut the tube on a 45°, rotate your ruler match the edge of the ruler with the previously cut edge to form a point. Cut again to create a triangle. Continue cutting until you have 5 triangles cut from the tube. Repeat with remaining strip sets.

3 Remove any stitches at the triangle's point if necessary and open to reveal a pieced square unit. Press each unit toward the darker fabric.

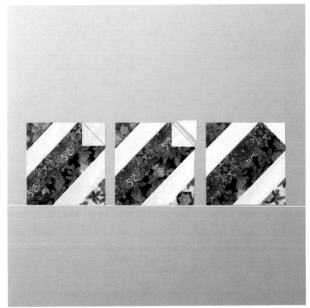

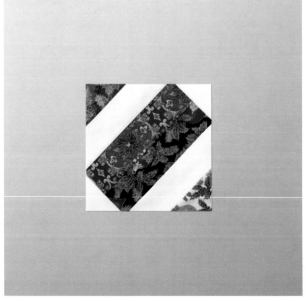

4 Mark a diagonal line on the reverse side of a background square. Lay the marked square on a corner of the block and sew across the marked line. Trim the excess fabric and press the snowballed corner toward the background fabric.

5 Repeat to snowball the opposite corner of the square unit to complete the block. Make 42 blocks.

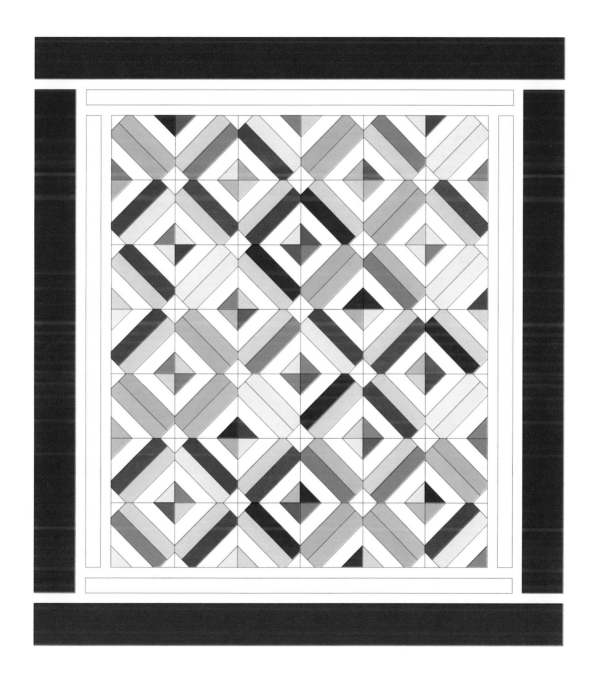

For the tutorial and everything you need to make this quilt visit:
www.msqc.co/holidayblock19

snowballed disappearing four-patch

My love of sewing began with a love of the theater. In high school, I was a regular in Drama Club and sang in musicals. Alongside that hobby, I soon began sewing my own costumes. Years later, as a young mother, I indulged my love of costuming every year when Halloween would roll around. It was a treat to help dress up my kids in darling costumes that I made especially for them. They paraded around town, gathering up candy as witches, scarecrows, mummies, superheroes, monsters, ghosts, and anything else their little minds could dream up.

When I was little, in the 1960s, costumes were much simpler. They weren't the fancy store-bought costumes you see today, but were made from whatever you might find around the house. Cardboard tissue boxes became big feet for Frankenstein's monster, sheets became ghosts, and Dad's suspenders held up oversized clown pants. If Mom was willing, she might powder your face and add rouge to your cheeks for the final touch. Last Halloween, I was astounded at the array of costumes with incredible details that I saw. I had a parade of children ringing my doorbell dressed as dinosaurs, pirates, princesses, villains, video game characters, movie stars, and sports heroes, but no costume was more popular than unicorns. Can you believe that? I was tickled pink!

As I encountered precious unicorns all Halloween night long, I couldn't help but smile as they whinnied and pranced in their iridescent pastel costumes. Myself, I am a fan of unicorns and I'm happy to see that they're making a comeback. When my girls were little, there were so many cute cartoons, books, and movies about unicorns, not to mention toy unicorns of every shape, size, and color. There was an entire generation of youth who were enthralled by them. There's just something magical about their majestic spiral horns, windblown mane, and shiny hooves. Now, they're as popular as ever.

Unicorns have captivated us for centuries. The Greek historian Ctesias wrote about these mythical creatures in the 5th century BCE saying they had white bodies, purple heads, blue eyes, and a multicolored horn. Over a thousand years later, Marco Polo thought he had discovered unicorns on his travels and said, "They spend their time by preference wallowing in mud and slime. They are very ugly brutes to look at. They are not at all such as we describe unicorns." But it turns out he was actually talking about rhinoceroses! Even the infamous Genghis Khan claimed to have encountered a unicorn. He said that it bowed to him, which caused him to change his mind about conquering India, so he turned his army right around.

I think what I like most about unicorns is that they symbolize goodness and purity. They remind us that we can be strong and courageous, just like them. When I put on a costume, I like to take on the persona of whatever I'm wearing, and if I were wearing a unicorn horn, I imagine I'd feel very powerful!

materials

QUILT SIZE
57" x 65"

BLOCK SIZE
8" finished

SUPPLY LIST
2 packages of 5" print squares
2¼ yards background fabric

BORDER
1 yard

BINDING
¾ yard

BACKING
3¾ yards - horizontal seam(s)

SAMPLE QUILT
Costume Maker's Ball by Janet
Wecker Frisch for Riley Blake Designs

1 cut

From the background fabric, cut:

- (11) 5″ strips across the width of the fabric. Subcut the strips into 5″ squares. Each strip will yield 8 squares and a **total of 84** are needed.

- (7) 3″ strips across the width of the fabric. Subcut the strips into 3″ squares. Each strip will yield 13 squares and a **total of 84** are needed.

2 make 4-patches

Pick up 2 different print squares and 2 background squares. Arrange them in a 4-patch formation, making sure the background squares are not next to each another. Sew the squares together in rows. Press the seam of the top row to the right and the bottom row to the left. Nest the seams and sew the 2 rows together to complete the 4-patch block. **Make 42. 2A**

3 cut, shuffle, sew

Cut the sewn block twice horizontally and twice vertically. Use the center seam as a guide and measure 1½″ out. Cut on either side of both center seams. **3A**

Swap the first and last blocks in the top row. Swap the first and last blocks in the bottom row. Rotate the 4-patch in the center of the middle row 90° so that the prints within the 4-patch are touching the matching print in the corner of the block. **3B**

Sew the squares together in rows. Press the seams of the top and bottom rows to the right and the center row to the left. Sew the rows together. **3C**

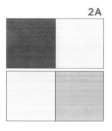

2A

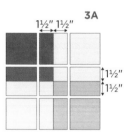

3A

1½″ 1½″   1½″ 1½″

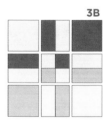

3B

3C

4 snowball
the corners

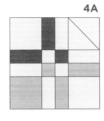

4A

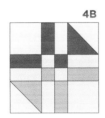

4B

Mark the diagonal on the reverse side of each of the 3″ background squares. Place a marked background square right sides facing on top of 1 of the print squares in the corner of the block. Sew on the marked line. Trim away the excess fabric leaving a ¼″ seam allowance. Press toward the snowballed corner. **4A**

Repeat to snowball the remaining print corner of the block. Trim the block to 8½″ if necessary. **4B**

Make 42 blocks.
Block Size: 8″ finished

5 arrange & sew

Lay out the blocks in rows. Each row is made up of **6 blocks** and **7 rows** are needed. After the blocks have been sewn into rows, press the seam allowances of the odd rows toward the right and the even rows toward the left to make the seams nest.

Sew the rows together to complete the center of the quilt.

6 border

From the outer border fabric, cut (6) 5″ strips across the width of the fabric. Sew the strips together end-to-end to make 1 long strip. Trim the borders from this strip.

Refer to Borders (pg. 110) in the Construction Basics to measure and cut the outer borders. The strips are approximately 56½″ for the sides and 57½″ for the top and bottom.

7 quilt & bind

Layer the quilt with batting and backing and quilt. After the quilting is complete, square up the quilt and trim away all excess batting and backing. Add binding to complete the quilt. See Construction Basics (pg. 110) for binding instructions.

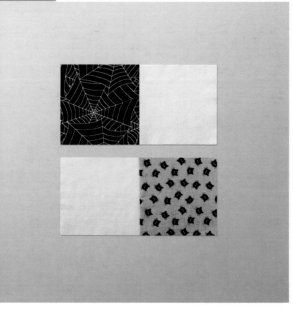

1 Arrange 2 background and 2 print squares in 2 rows of 2 with the background squares in opposing corners. Sew the squares together in rows and press the seams in opposite directions. Nest the seams and sew the 2 rows together to complete the 4-patch.

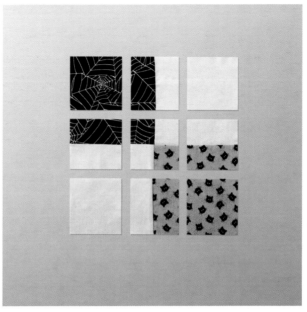

2 Cut the 4-patch twice horizontally, 1½" on either side of the center seam. Cut the 4-patch twice vertically, 1½" on either side of the center seam to yield 9 pieces.

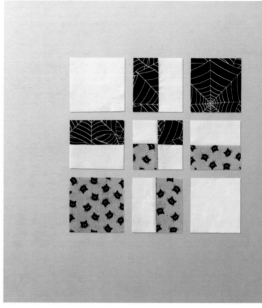

3 Swap the locations of the first and last squares in the top row. Do the same with the first and last squares in the bottom row. Rotate the 4-patch in the center of the block 90°. Sew the pieces of the block back together in this arrangement.

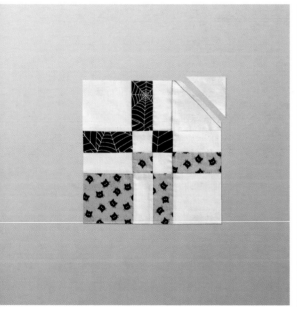

4 Mark a diagonal line on the reverse side of a 3" background square. Lay the marked square on a print corner of the block. Sew on the marked line and trim away the excess fabric.

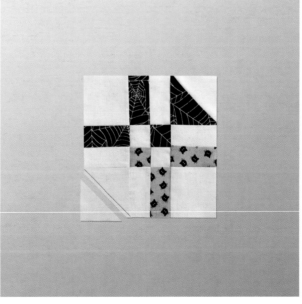

5 Mark a diagonal line on another 3" background square and use it to snowball the print square in the opposite corner of the block. Trim the excess fabric ¼" away from the seam.

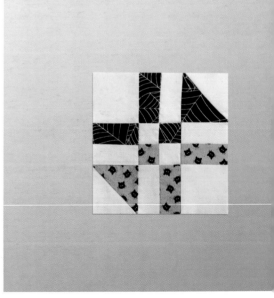

6 Press toward the snowballed corner to complete the block. Repeat to make 42 blocks.

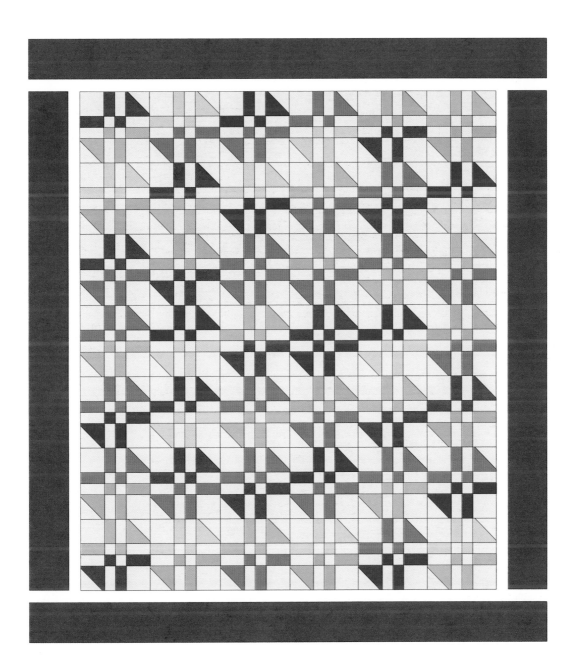

diamond chain

Mandy couldn't believe her rotten luck. It was Thanksgiving Day and she felt absolutely miserable. She'd been excited for weeks to celebrate with her family. In fact, because both her parents and her in-laws lived so close, she and her husband spent the holiday at both parents' houses. Eating Thanksgiving dinner twice was a challenge she was usually willing to accept! But not this year. As soon as she got out of bed, she wanted to get right back in and curl up under the covers. The room spun. She felt nauseous and dizzy. Getting the flu on Thanksgiving was the worst timing she could imagine. She'd have to stay home and miss out on the feast.

Mandy spent the morning lying on the couch, watching the Macy's Thanksgiving Day Parade on TV, but by the afternoon, she started to perk up. After a hot shower, she almost felt like herself again. When she checked her temperature, nothing seemed amiss, so with renewed vigor, she dressed herself and announced to her husband that they would be able to go to dinner after all! He packed up the pies and they headed up to his parents' house.

As soon as Mandy walked in the door, she knew she wasn't okay. The scent of roasted turkey hit her nostrils like a Mack truck and she retched. Oh no. It was back again! She nibbled on rolls and sipped 7-Up while the rest of the family ate generous portions of stuffing, mashed potatoes, and yams, but nothing appealed to her. Not even the green Jell-o salad with mini marshmallows, her favorite.

During dessert, she skipped the pumpkin pie. Just the thought of its mushy texture made her retreat to the living room to hide under a quilt.

While driving home after the festivities were over, Mandy suddenly realized she felt better, but the next morning, it was all back again. Doing a quick calculation in her head, Mandy realized she most likely didn't have the flu. After confirming it herself with a test, she told her husband the news when he got home from work. "I'm pregnant!" His face lit up and they embraced. Then, she wondered aloud, "So, how do we tell the family?"

Christmas was just around the corner, and Mandy wanted to wait to tell everyone that morning. Knowing they would soon become grandparents would be the perfect gift for both of their parents. Their plan was to put a neckerchief on the dog that said, "I'm going to be a big brother!" and just see what happened.

On Christmas morning, they burst in the door along with the dog and let him loose. He sniffed around and nobody seemed to notice the news at first. But then, one by one, the siblings read the message on the dog's neckerchief and smiled. They shushed each other, waiting for their parents to notice. It took about a half hour until the cat was finally out of the bag! Everyone was thrilled and Mandy's unpredictable illness over Thanksgiving finally made sense.

For the tutorial and everything
you need to make this quilt visit:
www.msqc.co/holidayblock19

73

materials

QUILT SIZE
64" x 72"

BLOCK SIZE
8" finished

SUPPLIES
2 packages 5" print squares
2 packages 5" background squares

INNER BORDER
½ yard

OUTER BORDER
1½ yards

BINDING
¾ yard

BACKING
4½ yards - vertical seam(s)

SAMPLE QUILT
Winterberry by My Mind's Eye for Riley
Blake Designs

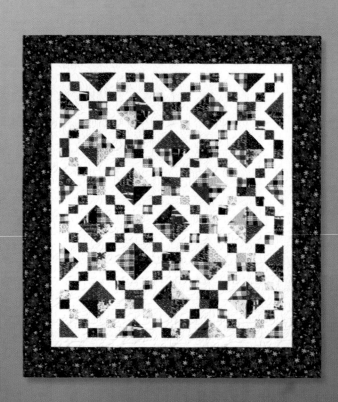

1 half-square triangles

Mark a diagonal line on the reverse side of a 42 background squares. Pair each marked background square with a print square, right sides together. Sew on both sides of the marked diagonal line using a ¼" seam allowance. Cut on the marked line and open to reveal 2 half-square triangles. Press toward the dark fabric. Square up to 4½". **1A**

Repeat to **make 84** half-square triangles.

2 make 4-patches

Pair a background square with a print square, right sides facing. Sew on 2 opposite sides of the squares. Measure 2½" from the edge of the sewn squares and cut. Press toward the dark fabric. **2A**

Repeat with all remaining background and print squares to yield 84 pieced units.

Select 2 pieced units that don't match. Place these 2 units together, right sides

facing. Make sure the center seams are aligned and the background fabrics are not on top of each other. Sew on the 2 opposing sides that cross the previously sewn seams. **2B**

Measure 2½" from the edge of the sewn squares and cut. Press to 1 side. **2C**

Make (84) 4-patches.

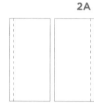
2A

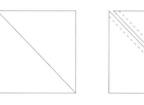

1A

2B

2C

3 block construction

Pick up 2 half-square triangles and (2) 4-patches. Arrange the units in a 4-patch formation as shown. **3A**

Sew the 2 units in the top row together and press the seam to the right. Sew the 2 units in the bottom row together and press the seam to the left. Nest the seams and sew the 2 rows together to complete the block.

Make 42 blocks.
Block Size: 8″ finished

3A

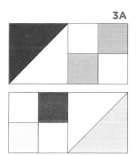

4 arrange & sew

Lay out the blocks in rows making note of the block orientation in the diagram on page 79. Each row is made up of **6 blocks** and **7 rows** are needed. After the blocks have been sewn into rows, press the seam allowances of the odd rows toward the right and the even rows toward the left to make the seams nest.

Sew the rows together to complete the center of the quilt.

5 inner border

From the inner border fabric, cut (6) 2½″ strips across the width of the fabric. Sew the strips together end-to-end to make 1 long strip. Trim the borders from this strip.

Refer to Borders (pg. 110) in the Construction Basics to measure and cut the inner borders. The strips are approximately 56½″ for the sides and 52½″ for the top and bottom.

6 outer border

From the outer border fabric, cut (7) 6½″ strips across the width of the fabric. Sew the strips together end-to-end to make 1 long strip. Trim the borders from this strip.

Refer to Borders (pg. 110) in the Construction Basics to measure and cut the outer borders. The strips are approximately 60½″ for the sides and 64½″ for the top and bottom.

7 quilt & bind

Layer the quilt with batting and backing and quilt. After the quilting is complete, square up the quilt and trim away all excess batting and backing. Add binding to complete the quilt. See Construction Basics (pg. 110) for binding instructions.

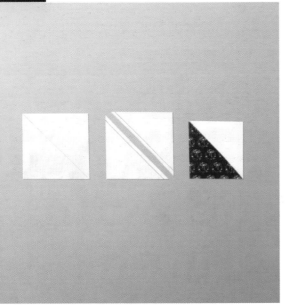

1 Mark a diagonal line on the reverse side of a background square. Lay the marked square with a print square, right sides facing. Sew on both sides of the marked line using a ¼" seam allowance. Cut on the marked line and open to reveal 2 half-square triangles. Square up to 4½". Make 84.

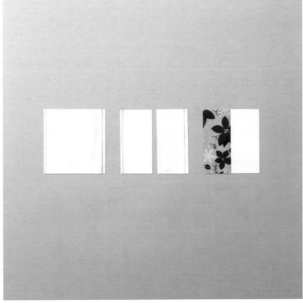

2 Layer a background square with a print square right sides together. Sew on 2 opposing sides. Measure 2½" from the square's edge and cut parallel to the seams. Press away from the background fabric. Make 84 units.

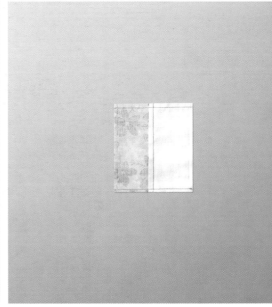

3 Place 2 nonmatching units right sides together, nest the seams, and make sure the background fabrics in each unit are not on top of each other. Sew on 2 opposite sides, crossing the previously sewn seams.

4 Measure 2½" from the square's edge and cut parallel to the last seams sewn. Press to 1 side. Make 84.

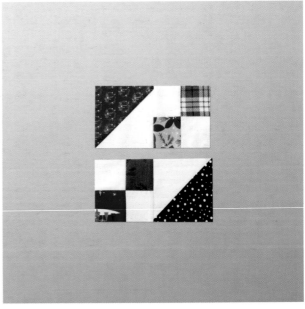

5 Select 2 half-square triangles and (2) 4-patches and arrange them in 2 rows of 2 as shown. Sew together in rows. Press the seam in the top row to the right and the bottom row to the left. Nest the seams and sew the top and bottom rows together to complete the block. Make 42.

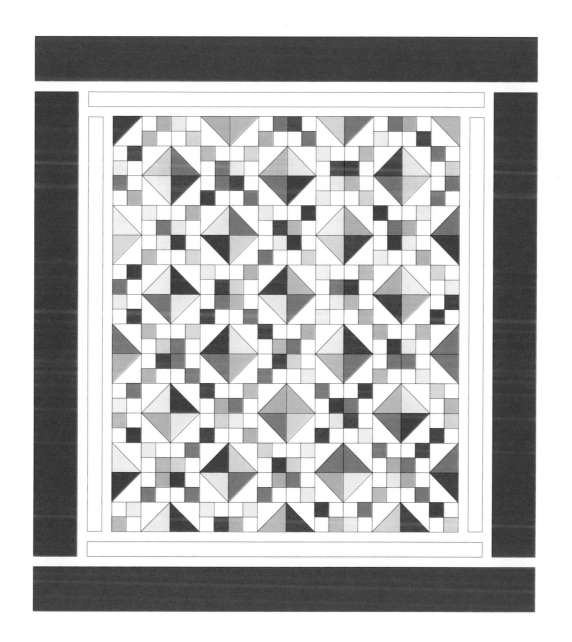

For the tutorial and everything
you need to make this quilt visit:
www.msqc.co/holidayblock19

80

inside out heart

Firsts are so exciting. All the anticipation leading up to one unforgettable moment, along with the thrill of the unknown, makes it so special. Remember the first day of school? Your first time riding a bicycle? A baby's first steps? The first time flying on an airplane? The first night in a new house? Your first job? That first love? And your first kiss? These moments are filled with mixed emotions and they don't always turn out quite the way we imagine them, but they lay a foundation for what comes next. After all, if your first attempt doesn't turn out quite right, there are plenty more opportunities to keep learning!

At nearly 30 years old, Sam had never had a serious girlfriend until that time. He had met his new girlfriend, Cindy, on a blind date. It all came about because Sam and Cindy's mothers were friends. They had a feeling their children might get along (and wouldn't it be fun to be in-laws!), so they gently nudged the pair together until Sam somehow had Cindy's phone number and she had his. He called her and quickly asked her out. Within two minutes the call was over, but she'd said yes!

He picked her up in his freshly vacuumed Honda and they went to play mini golf and have ice cream. They putt-putted while they chatted about life and soon found out that they had a lot in common. In fact, they lived only ten minutes away from each other most of their lives. They even attended the same high school and college, but because Sam was a few years younger, they had never

crossed paths before. By the time they were eating ice cream, they'd taken a shine to each other and decided to meet up the next day. And the next. And the next.

As their relationship grew, so did Sam's apprehension about one tiny thing—he'd never kissed anyone before! Each night, as Sam hugged Cindy goodbye, leaning on his car, he couldn't muster up the courage to kiss her goodnight. The next time they spoke, he blurted out his dilemma and she let out a deep laugh. "You've never been kissed?" she asked. He reluctantly admitted that he hadn't. Thankfully, her solution was simple. "Well, the next time you see me, just kiss me!" He tentatively agreed and she said she'd be over the next morning during her break.

Cindy drove a school bus and didn't have any routes mid-morning, so she usually went over to Sam's house and they had an early lunch together before her afternoon route. This morning, she went right over to his house and found him waiting at the door. Before he could invite her inside, she kissed him right then and there, standing on the front doorstep! It took him by surprise, but he was relieved to have that first kiss out of the way. There were plenty more kisses after the first one, but he'd never forget it. Almost a year later, they were married. And he never had to worry about first kisses ever again!

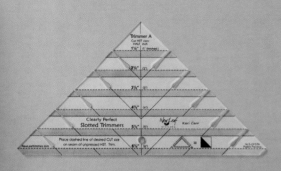

materials

QUILT SIZE
36" x 36"

BLOCK SIZE
6" finished

QUILT TOP
1 package 10" solid squares
1 package 10" background squares

BINDING
½ yard

BACKING
1¼ yards – vertical seam(s)

OTHER
Clearly Perfect Slotted Trimmer A

SAMPLE QUILT
Kona Cotton - Wildberry Palette by
Robert Kaufman Fabrics

1 cut

Select (6) 10″ background squares. Set the rest of the package of squares aside for the moment. Trim the 6 squares to 6½″ and set them aside until you are ready to lay out the quilt top.

2A

2 sew

Layer a 10″ background square right sides together with a solid square. Sew around the layered squares on all 4 sides using a ¼″ seam allowance. **2A**

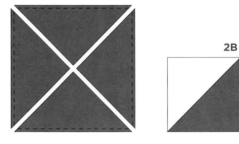

2B

Cut the sewn squares on both diagonals. Trim to 6½″ using the Clearly Perfect Slotted Trimmer A. While you're in the process of trimming, use the slots provided to trim off the dog ears. Open and press toward the darker fabric. Each pair of 10″ squares will yield 4 half-square triangles. Repeat with a second pair of 10″ squares to yield a **total of 8** half-square triangles. **2B**

Block Size: 6″ finished

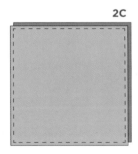

2C

Layer 2 different colored solid squares right sides together. Sew around the layered squares on all 4 sides using a ¼″ seam allowance. **2C**

Cut the sewn squares on both diagonals. Trim to 6½" using the Clearly Perfect Slotted Trimmer A. While you're in the process of trimming, use the slots provided to trim off the dog ears. Open and press toward the darker fabric.

Each pair of 10" squares will yield 4 half-square triangles. Repeat with 5 additional pairs of 10" squares. You will need a **total of 22** half-square triangles. Set the 2 extra half-square triangles and remaining 10" squares aside for another project. **2D**

Block Size: 6" finished

3 arrange & sew

Lay out the 6½" background squares and blocks in **6 rows of 6**, making note of the orientation of the blocks in the diagram on page 87. After the blocks have been sewn into rows, press the seam allowances of the odd rows toward the right and the even rows toward the left to make the seams nest.

Sew the rows together to complete the quilt top.

4 quilt & bind

Layer the quilt with batting and backing and quilt. After the quilting is complete, square up the quilt and trim away all excess batting and backing. Add binding to complete the quilt. See Construction Basics (pg. 110) for binding instructions.

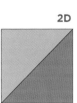

2D

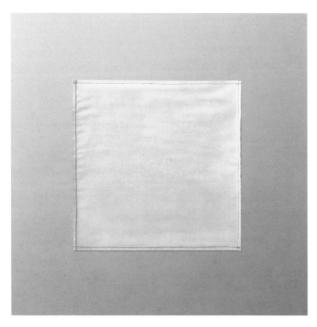

1 Layer a 10" background square and a 10" solid square together, right sides facing. Sew on all 4 sides using a ¼" seam allowance.

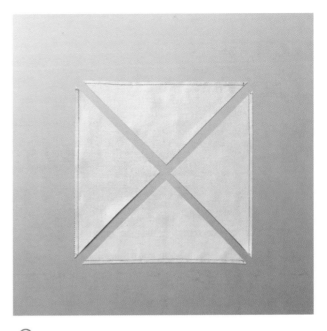

2 Cut the sewn squares on both diagonals to yield 4 units.

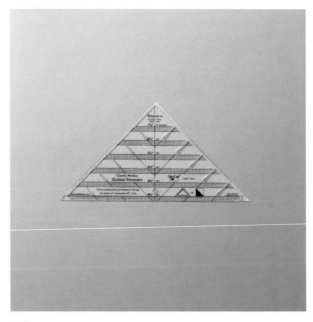

3 Use the Clearly Perfect Slotted Trimmer A to trim each unit to 6½".

4 Open each unit to reveal a half-square triangle. Press toward the darker fabric.

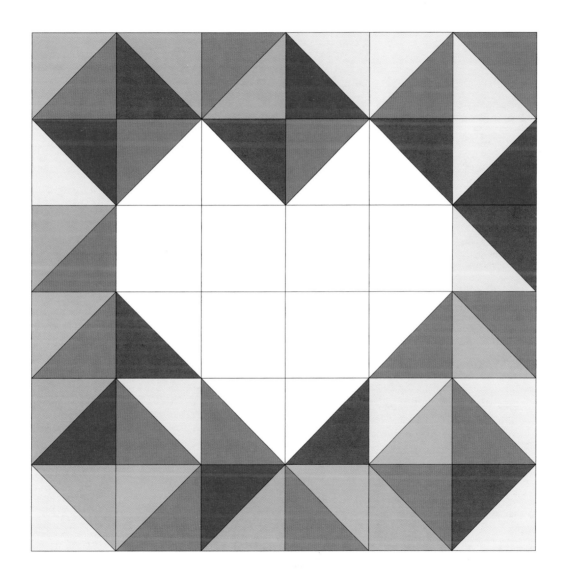

home for the holidays

five handmade gifts for any occasion

Adorn your home with handmade decorations to make every holiday special. These customizable projects come together quickly and create a festive atmosphere instantly! Celebrate the best of each season and make creative gifts for your loved ones they're sure to adore.

Celebrating holidays gives me something to look forward to all year long. I love the preparation up to the big day and thoughtful little details make each holiday even more memorable. As each holiday approaches, I pick through my fabric collection and ponder what decorations I might create—and these little projects come together so quickly! Even if you procrastinate, which I am occasionally guilty of, you could whip something together the night before and nobody would be the wiser!

Start out the year with a cute tumbler container to hold all your Valentine's Day cards or fill it with candy to hand out to loved ones! When the 4th of July rolls around, create a set of handy pot holders to keep your hands safe when you're doing all that delicious cooking. Then, as the fall season begins, adorn your home with ghostly pillows to welcome in the Halloween spirit. For Thanksgiving, a set of matching fabric bowl covers will wow your guests. And finally, at Christmastime, use up all your scraps to make thoughtful holiday cards to send to your family and friends! All of these fun, customizable projects make celebrating year-round a joy.

.

christmas cards

supplies

Scrap of fabric for the postcard front that measures at least 5" x 7"
Scrap of light colored solid fabric for the postcard back that measures at least 4" x 6"
(1) 4" x 6" rectangle of Timtex Stabilizer
Scrap of low loft batting that measures at least 5" x 7"

Optional Supplies:
Lightweight fusible web
Additional fabric as desired
Ribbon or other embellishments

Sample Project: Sweet Christmas by Urban Chiks for Moda Fabrics

cut & sew

Create your very own fabric postcard for any special occasion and it can actually be sent through the mail! This project begins by selecting your background fabric. If you have a larger scrap of fabric for your postcard front, you can choose your favorite motif within that fabric and fussy cut a 5" x 7" rectangle around it to feature it.

If you'd like to get a little fancier, you may add additional fabric shapes with fusible web to create a custom design. Follow the manufacturer's instructions on your fusible web to adhere it to the wrong side of your fabric. Cut out any motifs or shapes you like and fuse them onto the front of your postcard.

Once you have created a design you like for the front of your postcard, create a quilt sandwich by layering the postcard front on top of the batting with the Timtex on the bottom. Be sure the Timtex is in the center of the batting and fabric.

Quilt as you like. You can do some straight-line stitching, use your machine's decorative stitches, or drop the feed dogs and free-motion quilt. Be sure to stitch around the edges of any pieces you may have added with fusible web to be certain they'll stay in place.

When you've completed the quilting, turn the postcard over and trim all the layers to match the 4" x 6" rectangle of Timtex.

Layer the solid fabric for the postcard back against the Timtex. Set your sewing machine to do a satin stitch and sew around all the edges to finish your postcard. Make sure the needle goes just off the edge of the postcard on one side of the stitch but pierces the postcard on the other. You may find you need to go around the edges more than once to fill in all the spaces. When you're through, add any embellishments that can't be quilted.

pot holders

supplies

1 package of 5" squares (1 package of 5" squares is enough to make 10 potholder fronts)
10" square for backing
10" square of Insul-Bright
10" square of 100% cotton batting
1 fat quarter for binding

Sample Project: Back Porch Celebration by Meg Hawkey of Crabapple Hill for Maywood Studio

cut & sew

Layer (2) 5" squares with right sides facing. Sew on 2 opposite sides with a ¼" seam allowance. Measure 2½" from the outer edge and cut once between the seams. Open and press toward the darker fabric. Repeat with a second pair of 5" squares. **1A**

Pair 2 units using different fabrics from above. Nest the seams and sew on 2 opposite sides of the squares crossing the previously sewn seams. Measure 2½" from the outer edge and cut once between the seams. **1B**

Open to reveal a 4-patch unit and press to 1 side. Repeat to make (4) 4-patch units. **1C**

Arrange the 4-patch units in 2 rows of 2. Sew 2 units together to make a row. Press the seams of the upper row to the right and the lower row to the left. Nest the seams and sew the rows together to make the block.

Layer the pieces of the potholder together. Begin with the backing (wrong side up) then add the Insul-Bright, cotton batting, and the top of the potholder (right side up).

Pin the layers together to stabilize them and quilt as you wish. Trim the layers even with the potholder top.

Cut the fat quarter into 2¼" wide strips on the bias. After you've cut the strips, follow the Construction Basics (pg. 110) to sew the strips into 1 long strip. Fold the long strip in half with wrong sides together and press. Stitch the binding to the front of the potholder, then whipstitch it to the back.

NOTE: You will have enough binding to be able to join the 2 ends and make a loop for hanging if you choose.

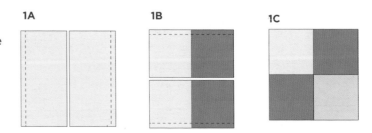

1A   1B   1C

bowl cover

Fits a 10" bowl

supplies
(2) 18" squares of fabric
(1) 18" square fusible fleece
(1) 30" length of ¼" elastic

Sample Project: Give Thanks II by Art for Bernie for Blank Quilting

prepare

Follow the manufacturer's instructions to adhere the fusible fleece to the reverse side of 1 of the fabric squares.

Fold the remaining 18" fabric square in half horizontally and vertically to find the center of the square. Press to mark the center. Open the square and lay it out flat. Draw a 16" diameter circle by measuring 8" from the center point and marking every inch or so around the circumference of the circle. **1A**

Connect the marks you made and cut along the curved edge.

Lay the cut circle on top of the other fabric/fusible fleece square. Trace around the circumference of the circle and cut the fabric/fusible fleece square on that traced line.

sew

Layer the circles with the right sides of fabric facing and sew around the edge of the circle using a ½" seam allowance. Leave an opening of 3-4". **2A**

Clip the curves and turn right side out. Press.

Topstitch around the entire circle with a ½" seam allowance to create a channel for the elastic.

Attach a small safety pin to the end of the elastic and feed it through the channel. Once you've fed the elastic through, remove the safety pin and make sure the elastic is not twisted. Overlap the elastic ends by about 1" and use a zigzag stitch to stitch across each end.

Tuck the elastic and seam allowance inside the channel and whipstitch the opening closed.

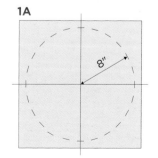

1A

2A

ghost pillow cover

Fits a 16″ pillow form

supplies
½ yard black fabric
1 fat quarter white fabric
¼ yard Heat n Bond Lite
(1) 16″ pillow form

Sample Project: So Adora-Boo! By Ryan Conners for Blank Quilting and Bella Solids – White by Moda Fabrics

cut
From the black fabric, cut (1) 18″ square and (2) 10″ x 17″ rectangles.

appliqué
Make a copy of the templates and increase them 200%. Trace the appliqué pieces onto the paper side of the fusible web. Keep in mind that everything you trace will be reversed. Roughly cut out the pieces, leaving a generous amount of space around the outer edges.

Follow the manufacturer's instructions and adhere the fusible web to the reverse side of the white fabric for the ghost and black fabric for the eyes and mouth.

Using a sharp pair of scissors, cut out each of the appliqué pieces.

Remove the paper backing from the ghost body and position it in the center of the 18″ square of black fabric. Remove the paper backing from the ghost's eyes and mouth and place them on top of the body. When you're happy with the placement, follow the manufacturer's instructions to adhere the ghost in place.

Stitch around the ghost body, eyes, and mouth using a buttonhole stitch and matching thread.

After you have completed the appliqué work, press and trim the square to 17″.

sew
To make the pillow back, turn (1) 17″ side of a 10″ x 17″ rectangle under ¼″ and press. Turn the same side of the rectangle under another ¼″ and press again. Topstitch across the turned edge. Repeat for remaining rectangle.

Align the raw edges of the rectangles with the front of the pillow top with right sides facing. The 2 rectangles of the pillow back will overlap by about 3″. Stitch around the outer edge with a ½″ seam allowance. **3A**

Turn the pillow cover right side out and insert the pillow form to complete the project.

3A

bottom flap

scrap basket

supplies

(10) 10" fabric squares
(1) package Bosal In-R-Form Plus Double Sided Fusible Foam Stabilizer
(1) 2½" x 40" strip of fabric for binding
Missouri Star Quilt Co. Large Tumbler Template

Sample Project: Love Struck by Shelly Comiskey for Henry Glass

prepare

From the 10" fabric squares, cut (8) side pieces using the template. 4 side pieces will be for the exterior and 4 side pieces will be for the lining. From the remaining 10" fabric squares, cut (2) 6" squares.

From the Bosal Fusible, cut 4 side pieces using the template and (1) 6" square.

sew

Follow the manufacturer's instructions to fuse a fabric side piece to either side of a side stabilizer piece. The reverse side of the fabric will face the stabilizer. Repeat to fuse the 6" fabric squares to the square of stabilizer.

Sew each of the side pieces to the 6" square using a zigzag stitch. **2A**

Sew the side seams together using a zigzag stitch. The seams will be on the outside edges, so if you would prefer, use a decorative stitch. **2B**

Fold the 2½" wide strip of fabric in half with wrong sides touching and press. Align the raw edge with the top of the basket on the outside edge and stitch in place. Flip the binding to the inner edge and sew. **2C**

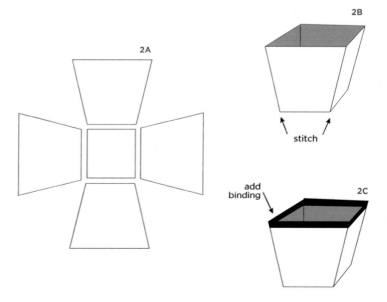

christmas tree pinwheel

QUILT SIZE
73" x 81"

BLOCK SIZE
8" finished

SUPPLIES
1 package of 10" assorted green squares
3½ yards background fabric
¼ yard brown fabric
¼ yard yellow fabric

BORDER
1¼ yards

BINDING
¾ yard

BACKING
5 yards - vertical seam(s)

SAMPLE QUILT
Wilmington Essentials - Emerald Forest
10 Karat Gems for Wilmington Prints

QUILTING PATTERN
Pine Tree Meander

ONLINE TUTORIALS
msqc.co/holidayblock19

PATTERN
pg. 6

disappearing
hourglass
crazy eight

QUILT SIZE
82½" x 93¾"

BLOCK SIZE
11¼" finished

QUILT TOP
1 package 10" print squares
1 package 10" black squares

OUTER BORDER
¾ yard

OUTER BORDER
1¾ yards

BINDING
¾ yard

BACKING
8½ yards - vertical seam(s)
    or 3 yards of 108" wide

SAMPLE QUILT
Autumn Time by Color Principle for
Henry Glass

QUILTING PATTERN
Leaves

ONLINE TUTORIALS
msqc.co/holidayblock19

PATTERN
pg. 14

geese in motion

QUILT SIZE
73" x 70½"

QUILT TOP
1 roll of 2½" print strips
2 yards background fabric
  – includes inner border

OUTER BORDER
1¼ yards

BINDING
¾ yard

BACKING
4½ yards – vertical seam(s)

OTHER
Binding Tool by TQM Products

SAMPLE QUILT
Nova by BasicGrey for Moda Fabrics

QUILTING PATTERN
Christmas Paisley

ONLINE TUTORIALS
msqc.co/holidayblock19

PATTERN
pg. 22

spring twist

QUILT SIZE
63" x 69"

BLOCK SIZE
6" finished

QUILT TOP
1 roll 2½" print strips
1¼ yards complementary fabric
   - includes inner border

OUTER BORDER
1¼ yards

BINDING
¾ yard

BACKING
4¼ yards – vertical seam(s)

SAMPLE QUILT
Artisan Batiks Cornucopia 10 by Lunn
Studios for Robert Kaufman

QUILTING PATTERN
Leaves

ONLINE TUTORIALS
msqc.co/holidayblock19

PATTERN
pg. 30

diamond
pavers

QUILT SIZE
68" x 68"

BLOCK SIZE
9½" finished

QUILT TOP
1 package 10" print squares
1½ yards white fabric
1½ yards black fabric

BORDER
1¼ yards

BINDING
¾ yard

BACKING
4¼ yards – vertical seam(s)

SAMPLE QUILT
Ghostly Glow Town by Shelly Comiskey
for Henry Glass

QUILTING PATTERN
Ghostly

ONLINE TUTORIALS
msqc.co/holidayblock19

PATTERN
pg. 38

jenny's winter wall hanging

SIZE
48" x 42"

PROJECT TOP
1 package 10" print squares
1½ yards background fabric
   - includes inner border
¼ yard cuddle fabric

OUTER BORDER
¾ yard

BINDING
¾ yard

BACKING
3 yards - vertical seam(s)

OTHER
2 large buttons
Missouri Star Quilt Co.
   - Large Simple Wedge Template
   - Large Half-Hexagon Template

SAMPLE QUILT
The Joy of Giving by Susan Winget for
Wilmington Prints

QUILTING PATTERN
Holly

ONLINE TUTORIALS
msqc.co/holidayblock19

PATTERN
pg. 46

brick yard

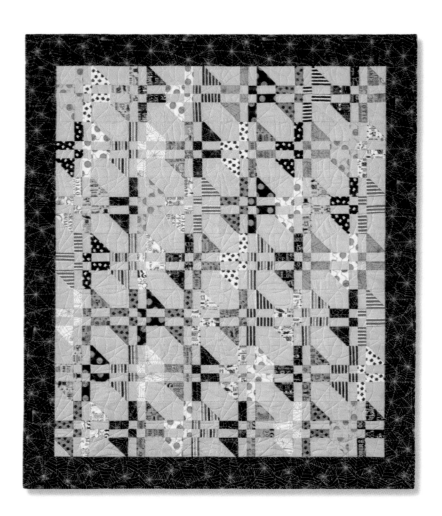

snowballed disappearing four-patch

QUILT SIZE
57" x 65"

BLOCK SIZE
8" finished

SUPPLY LIST
2 packages of 5" print squares
2¼ yards background fabric

BORDER
1 yard

BINDING
¾ yard

BACKING
3¾ yards - horizontal seam(s)

SAMPLE QUILT
Costume Maker's Ball by Janet
Wecker Frisch for Riley Blake Designs

QUILTING PATTERN
Spider Webs

ONLINE TUTORIALS
msqc.co/holidayblock19

PATTERN
pg. 64

diamond chain

QUILT SIZE
64" x 72"

BLOCK SIZE
8" finished

SUPPLIES
2 packages 5" print squares
2 packages 5" background squares

INNER BORDER
½ yard

OUTER BORDER
1½ yards

BINDING
¾ yard

BACKING
4½ yards - vertical seam(s)

SAMPLE QUILT
Winterberry by My Mind's Eye for
Riley Blake Designs

QUILTING PATTERN
Christmas Paisley

ONLINE TUTORIALS
msqc.co/holidayblock19

PATTERN
pg. 72

inside out heart

QUILT SIZE
36" x 36"

BLOCK SIZE
6" finished

QUILT TOP
1 package 10" solid squares
1 package 10" background squares

BINDING
½ yard

BACKING
1¼ yards – vertical seam(s)

OTHER
Clearly Perfect Slotted Trimmer A

SAMPLE QUILT
Kona Cotton - Wildberry Palette by
Robert Kaufman Fabrics

QUILTING PATTERN
Hearts

ONLINE TUTORIALS
msqc.co/holidayblock19

PATTERN
pg. 80

construction basics

general quilting

- All seams are ¼" inch unless directions specify differently.
- Cutting instructions are given at the point when cutting is required.
- Precuts are not prewashed; therefore do not prewash other fabrics in the project.
- All strips are cut width of fabric.
- Remove all selvages.

press seams

- Use a steam iron on the cotton setting.
- Press the seam just as it was sewn right sides together. This "sets" the seam.
- With dark fabric on top, lift the dark fabric and press back.
- The seam allowance is pressed toward the dark side. Some patterns may direct otherwise for certain situations.
- Follow pressing arrows in the diagrams when indicated.
- Press toward borders. Pieced borders may demand otherwise.
- Press diagonal seams open on binding to reduce bulk.

borders

- Always measure the quilt top 3 times before cutting borders.
- Start measuring about 4" in from each side and through the center vertically.
- Take the average of those 3 measurements.
- Cut 2 border strips to that size. Piece strips together if needed.
- Attach one to either side of the quilt.

- Position the border fabric on top as you sew. The feed dogs can act like rufflers. Having the border on top will prevent waviness and keep the quilt straight.
- Repeat this process for the top and bottom borders, measuring the width 3 times.
- Include the newly attached side borders in your measurements.
- Press toward the borders.

binding

find a video tutorial at: www.msqc.co/006

- Use 2½" strips for binding.
- Sew strips end-to-end into one long strip with diagonal seams, aka the plus sign method (next). Press seams open.
- Fold in half lengthwise wrong sides together and press.
- The entire length should equal the outside dimension of the quilt plus 15" - 20."

plus sign method

- Lay one strip across the other as if to make a plus sign right sides together.
- Sew from top inside to bottom outside corners crossing the intersections of fabric as you sew.
  Trim excess to ¼" seam allowance.
- Press seam open.

find a video tutorial at: www.msqc.co/001

attach binding

- Match raw edges of folded binding to the quilt top edge.
- Leave a 10" tail at the beginning.
- Use a ¼" seam allowance.
- Start in the middle of a long straight side.

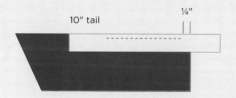

10" tail   ¼"

miter corners

- Stop sewing ¼" before the corner.
- Move the quilt out from under the presser foot.
- Clip the threads.
- Flip the binding up at a 90° angle to the edge just sewn.
- Fold the binding down along the next side to be sewn, aligning raw edges.
- The fold will lie along the edge just completed.
- Begin sewing on the fold.

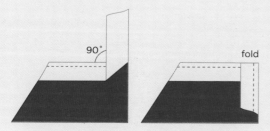

90°   fold

close binding

MSQC recommends The Binding Tool from TQM Products to finish binding perfectly every time.

- Stop sewing when you have 12" left to reach the start.
- Where the binding tails come together, trim excess leaving only 2½" of overlap.
- It helps to pin or clip the quilt together at the two points where the binding starts and stops. This takes the pressure off of the binding tails while you work.
- Use the plus sign method to sew the two binding ends together, except this time when making the plus sign, match the edges. Using a pencil, mark your sewing line because you won't be able to see where the corners intersect. Sew across.

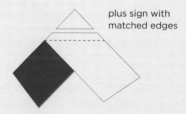

plus sign with matched edges

- Trim off excess; press seam open.
- Fold in half wrong sides together, and align all raw edges to the quilt top.
- Sew this last binding section to the quilt. Press.
- Turn the folded edge of the binding around to the back of the quilt and tack into place with an invisible stitch or machine stitch if you wish.